Hands On Social Studies

Grades 7-8

Melinda Scott
322½ Bill Edwards St.

Table of Contents

1

Economics

The Great Depression

Concepts

- The Great Depression was the longest period of high unemployment and low business activity in history.
- Many causes contributed to the Depression.
- President Roosevelt introduced many social reforms during this time to help ease the Depression.
- There was a lot of human suffering during the Great Depression.

Objectives

- To understand what the Great Depression was
- To understand the impact the Great Depression had on people's lives

Vocabulary

broker, corporations, dividend, Dow Jones, Federal Deposit Insurance Corporation (FDIC), Federal Reserve, foreclosure, hobo, interest rates, investments, margin, recession, Securities Exchange Commission (SEC), speculate, ticker tape

Preparation

Make a copy of page 4, *More for Your Money*, and a copy of the song, "Brother, Can You Spare A Dime?", on page 3 for each student.

Background Information

After World War I, businesses expanded. The stock market soared. Many people in the nation enjoyed prosperous times. Some celebrities of this time included Jack Dempsey, Al Capone, Charles Lindbergh and "Babe" Ruth. These good-time years were labeled the Roaring Twenties.

All of the good times changed in October of 1929 when investors lost confidence in the stock market. Stock prices fell drastically. Production and earnings fell. Wages fell. Banks failed.

People lost their jobs. Long unemployment and bread lines formed. The era of prosperity came to a grinding halt, and a period of poverty began.

Teaching Suggestions

- You know your students' background. If the students have not studied about the Great Depression, provide texts, encyclopedias and/or trade materials from which they may gain an understanding of the period.
- Before starting a discussion about the Depression, ask students what they know about the stock market. Go over the vocabulary with them to help them better understand the stock market. This will also help them see how the stock market was one factor of the Depression. Discuss what happened during the Twenties with students. Explain that this was a time for expansion and fun. Businesses boomed. Prohibition was in. Corporations needed money to build automated factories. They sold their shares in their companies. The stock market soared. Ask students what happened next.
- Tell students that the stock market fell over 500 points in one day in 1987, but no depression followed. However, explain to students that there is no guarantee that there will never be another depression. Ask students what changes were made because of the 1929 crash. (Federal Reserve controls percentage of margin, SEC, computers used instead of ticker tape.) Have students write stories pretending another depression did follow the 1987 loss of over 500 points. Students should write how their lives changed, what times are like now, etc.
- Arrange for a field trip to a brokerage house.
- Explain to students that the fallen stock market was not the only cause of the Depression. Ask them what happened to over 9,000 banks and why. (The banks closed from January 1930 to March 1933.)
- Ask how many students have bank accounts. Ask students how they might feel if they went to the bank after school and there was a sign saying, "CLOSED—OUT OF BUSINESS." Ask students what protection has been taken so that they won't lose their money. (FDIC)
- Ask students what happened to the farms, factories and stores. (Many failed due to lack of demand.) Ask students why this happened.
- As a review and to create a mental picture of the causes and effects of the Depression, have students list the causes of the Depression. Next to each cause, students should list an effect. This is a good group activity. Compare students' causes and effects.
- Ask students what they think life was like for many families during the Depression (i.e. where and how some lived; what people ate; what they did for work; what Hoovervilles were—shabby sections of town where people built shacks from flattened tin cans, etc.). Have students depict this on a mural.
- Have students write a page in a diary pretending that they just found out that the wage earner(s) in their family just lost his/her job.
- Ask students when things changed for the better. Ask what some of the changes were that President Roosevelt introduced. (New Deal—help for needy, more jobs created, businesses encouraged, laws made to reform businesses and government) Ask students how these changes helped. Ask students how Presidents Roosevelt and Hoover differed. (Hoover believed that if business was left alone to operate without government supervision, economic conditions would improve. Roosevelt wanted the federal government to fight the Depression.) Have students complete a Venn diagram on these two men or on two other aspects of the Depression.

The Great Depression continued

Economics

Teaching . . . continued

(A Venn diagram consists of two overlapping circles with characteristics unique to each subject in the non-overlapped areas and shared characteristics in the overlapped area.)

- Divide students into small groups. Have each group research a different program of reform enacted during Roosevelt's administration. Students can look them up under New Deal and/or by each specific name (i.e. Agricultural Adjustment Administration, Civilian Conservation Corps, Federal Emergency Relief Administration, FDIC, National Recovery Administration, Works Progress Administration, SEC, Tennessee Valley Authority, Public Works Administration, etc.).

- As you distribute copies of "Brother, Can You Spare A Dime?" below, tell the class that many songs were written during the Depression that told about the hard times. This song is probably the best known. Go over the words of the song and their meaning with the students. Instruct them to write a song to a familiar tune or a poem describing a hard time. They may write about the Depression or a personal hard time.

- Pictures taken at the time of the Great Depression can give students a better understanding of what life was like at this time. Show students pictures taken during the Depression. Let each student choose one and pretend he/she took the picture. Have students describe what is happening in the picture.

"Brother, Can You Spare A Dime?"   music by Jay Gorney

They used to tell me I was building a dream,
And so I followed the mob.
When there was earth to plough or guns to bear,
I was always there, right on the job.
They used to tell me I was building a dream
With peace and glory ahead.
Why should I be standing in line, just waiting for bread?

Chorus:
Once I built a railroad, now it's done—
Brother, can you spare a dime?
Once I built a tower to the sun—
Brick and rivet and lime.
Once I built a tower, now it's done—
Brother, can you spare a dime?

Once in khaki suits, gee, we looked swell
Full of that Yankee Doodle de dum.
Half a million boots went sloggin' through hell,
I was the kid with the drum.

Say, don't you remember, they called me Al—
It was Al all the time.
Say, don't you remember, I'm your pal—
Brother, can you spare a dime?

More for Your Money

Name _____

Food was inexpensive during the Depression compared to the cost of food today. However, it was still difficult for people to buy groceries. Many people lived on bread and potatoes. Some were lucky if they ate once a day. Many suffered from hunger and malnutrition.

Listed below on the left are some foods and their approximate costs in 1933. The cost is listed in cents. Go to a local market. Write the present cost of each item on the line after each item.

Item	1933 Price
5 lbs sugar	$.27
5 lbs flour	.26
1 lb loaf of bread	.07
1 lb round steak	.26
1 lb chuck roast	.16
1 lb pork chops	.20
1 lb bacon	.23
1 lb butter	.28
1 lb margarine	.13
1 dozen eggs	.29
1 qt milk (delivered)	.10
1 dozen oranges	.27
10 lbs potatoes	.23
1 can tomatoes (16-17 oz)	.08
1 lb navy beans	.05
1 lb coffee	.26

Item	Price Now
5 lbs sugar	$ _____
5 lbs flour	_____
1 lb loaf of bread	_____
1 lb round steak	_____
1 lb chuck roast	_____
1 lb pork chops	_____
1 lb bacon	_____
1 lb butter	_____
1 lb margarine	_____
1 dozen eggs	_____
1 qt milk	_____
1 dozen oranges	_____
10 lbs potatoes	_____
1 can tomatoes (16-17 oz)	_____
1 lb navy beans	_____
1 lb coffee	_____

What are some of your observations? _____

_____

_____

Plan an identical meal for a family of four in 1933 and in this year.

Amount	Item	Cost in 1933	Cost Now
		$	$
	TOTAL	$	$

International Trade

Economics

Concepts

- Countries depend on each other for goods and services.
- Countries produce goods from their most available resources.
- A trade deficit occurs when a country imports more than it exports.
- Tariffs, import quotas and economic alliances (i.e. EEC and NAFTA) can affect world trade.
- Countries have different currencies.

Objectives

- To realize that countries depend on each other for goods and services
- To understand how tariffs, trade quotas and economic alliances can affect world trade
- To understand that countries have different currencies

Vocabulary

balance of payments, capitalism, communism, European Economic Community (EEC), exchange rate, import quota, North American Free Trade Agreement (NAFTA), productive resources (natural resources, capital, labor force, technology), socialism, tariff, trade deficit

Materials

copies of *The Wall Street Journal* and other financial publications

Preparation

Save articles from newspapers about U.S. trade and other articles about international trade. Buy *The Wall Street Journal* and/or *Barron's* and other financial publications. Set up a "financial library" in which students may browse. Make a copy of page 6 for each group of 3-4 students.

Background Information

The U.S. and other nations depend on each other for goods and services. It makes sense for each country to produce goods for which the materials are more accessible and to import goods for which the cost of production is excessive. Even though each side gains from such an arrangement, some countries have tried to control their world trade by producing many of their own goods and controlling the amount of imports for fear of becoming too dependent on other nations.

Two methods used to restrict trade are tariffs and import quotas. The European Economic Community (EEC) is a group of European nations that have joined together to form one market for their economic resources. Jointly, they are the largest producer in the world market. They have done away with tariffs affecting trade among themselves.

The North American Free Trade Agreement (NAFTA) is between Canada, the U.S. and Mexico. It is an agreement to lower the barriers so goods will move more freely between the three countries. It reduces tariffs. Agreements between nations such as these intend to raise the standard of living of their people and to ease economic policies between them.

Trade between countries involves the exchange of different kinds of currency. A country that owes money to another uses an international system of banking to exchange one currency for another. The price in dollars depends on the current exchange rate.

Teaching Suggestions

- Go over vocabulary with students.
- Ask students to make a list of the pros and cons of a country producing all the goods its people need. Have them do the same for a country which produces only those for which it has the productive resources. Discuss the lists.
- Ask students what a country should take into consideration before it sets up production for a good or service. (needs of people; availability of resources; who will produce; competition)
- Ask students what a country wants to avoid when it imports and exports (deficit) and how it can accomplish this (tariff, import quota, etc.).
- Divide students into groups of three or four. Give each group a copy of activity page 6. Assign a country to each group. Tell the groups to fill in the name of the country at the top of the page. Then, students are to research the economy of that country to complete the page. Let the groups share their findings.
- On the board, write the names of the countries you assigned students in the above activity. After each country, write its main product(s) and its needs. Have students conclude how countries can benefit from one another.
- Have students find world trade articles in newspapers and bring them to class. Add some of your own to them if more are needed or use yours to stimulate discussion. Hang the articles on a bulletin board in the "financial library."
- Teach students how to read the foreign exchange rate in *The Wall Street Journal*. Have each student write a word problem for a different country using the rate data. Create an activity page using students' problems. Give each student a copy and let him/her work the problems.
- Let students create a world product mural. On it, have students include pictures of various countries and products or wrappers from products produced in these countries. Let students add to the mural as they find more products produced in other countries.

_____'s *Economy*

Economics

Name _____

Fill in the blanks below with the correct data.

Natural resources_____

Main economic activity _____

Main manufacturing activity _____

Products _____

_____

Products made in country for its consumption _____

_____

Needs _____

_____

Exports_____

_____

Imports _____

_____

Main trading partners_____

_____

Monetary system _____

Is country well-located for trade with other countries? _____ How are goods best transported? _____

_____

Problems in economy _____

_____

_____

What does the country do, if anything, to ease the flow of trade? _____

_____

What does the country do, if anything, to restrict trade? _____

_____

Make a graph that shows the percentage of workers in each area of production.

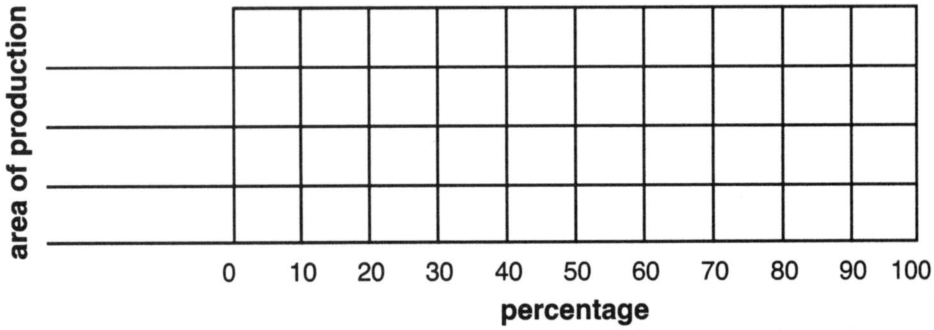

area of production

0   10   20   30   40   50   60   70   80   90   100

percentage

Capitalism

Concepts

- An economic system describes the way a nation produces and distributes goods and services.
- Capitalism, or the free enterprise system, is an economic system.
- The U.S. social, political and economic beliefs favor free enterprise.
- Individuals, businesses, the market, income and the government all play a part in a free enterprise system.
- In a free enterprise system, a person may own and market his/her business and compete with other like businesses to make a profit.
- Capitalism, communism, socialism and mixed economics are the four main types of economic systems.

Objectives

- To understand that anyone in our economic system has the right to own a business
- To realize that there are many hidden costs in a business
- To understand how supply and demand affect marketing
- To understand profit motive
- To see the need for some government control in free enterprise

Vocabulary

business, communism, corporation, economics, entrepreneur, management, market, net profit, partnerships, productive resources, profit motive, socialism

Materials

newspapers, magazines, penny candy, different kinds of candy, scissors, one copy of pages 9 and 10 per student

Background Information

Although students have contact with businesses, they do not necessarily understand how they are organized. There are millions of businesses in the U.S. They vary from small, single proprietorships to large corporations. No matter what these businesses produce—products or services—their goal is the same: to make a profit.

Teaching Suggestions

- Define different economic systems: capitalism (an economic system controlled chiefly by individuals and private companies instead of by the government), communism (government controls nearly all the resources used in production), socialism (national or local governments own and control a nation's resources), mixed economy (government owns some industries, private firms own others). Discuss with students whether they see any advantages or disadvantages in any of the systems.
- Ask the students which economic system the U.S. embraces. Have them cite examples to back their responses.
- Discuss some factors (underlined below) that influence economic decisions under capitalism. Ask some of the questions below and some of your own.
  Individuals: How do consumers influence the economy? How does the kind of job a person prepares for influence the economy? How do investors influence economic decisions?
  Businesses: What do businesses decide that influence the economy? How do businesses' quest for profit influence the economy?
  The Market: What helps set prices for products and services? How does supply and demand tend to change prices? What influence does competition have on the price and quality of products?
  Income: When may higher incomes be commanded?
  Government: What control does government have to maintain economic stability? What might happen if government did not control utilities? How does

government assure fair economic play? What are some economic programs for which government assumes responsibility?
- Write the following headings across the top of the chalkboard: Company, Small (50 or under), Large, Product, Service. Each should head a column. Ask students to name any company they know of and fill in the columns appropriately.
  Tell students that all businesses, large or small, have to be managed. Talk about the differences between a single proprietorship, partnerships and corporations.
  Give students an example of a product and/or service with which they are familiar (i.e. fast food establishment, bike, cleaners, TV repair, etc.). First, list with them the things that are needed to run a business that manufactures or produces one of the items or services (building, workers—be specific, equipment). Discuss with students whether a business runs more efficiently with more or less employees and why.
  Next, have students help you expand on the details of the business example you cited (i.e. rent, utilities, machinery, services—distribution, advertising, packaging, maintenance, marketing, training, production, customer service, etc.). Ask students why a business exists and how the components listed in the parentheses above affect its profit.
- Invite a business person to speak to your class about how his/her enterprise is run.
- Take a field trip to a business where students may observe every facet involved. Or, visit several neighborhood businesses where students may observe and possibly talk with owners/workers.
- Place several different kinds of "penny" candy on a table. Ask students which kind they would buy and why. Place several different kinds of candy (different

Capitalism continued

Teaching . . . continued

prices) on the table and ask students which kind they would buy and why. Talk about the factors which played a part in their decisions of choosing the candy. Ask them what businesses, which produce the same kinds of products, must do to be successful.

• Discuss with students the types of things businesses can do to be competitive.

• Write the names of business leaders (listed in *World Book*) on separate pieces of paper. Put them in a hat. Have each student draw a name and write a report about the person whose name he/she drew.

• The 50 leading U.S. manufacturers are listed in the *World Book*, but many more may be found in a variety of national business directories. Have students write a letter to a company requesting information on the history of the company, its product, production costs, distribution, profit, etc. Give students a large piece of paper on which to make a display that will give an overview of the company. Have them glue on items they want to include and tell them to write headlines or to outline items to which they want to call attention.

• Distribute activity page 9, *Consumer Choices*. Tell students to go through advertisements in newspapers and magazines and find at least two similar items. Have students cut them out and complete the page using what they know about the products.

After students have completed the page, divide them into groups. Instruct the groups to make up commercials for a product. Set time limits of 30 seconds or one minute for the commercials. Have students make the necessary backdrops and props. Videotape the commercials if possible and let students watch each other's.

• Distribute activity page 10, *Getting Started in a Business*. Go over it with students before they do it independently.

• Using a Venn diagram, have students compare two economic systems. In a Venn diagram, characteristics unique to each system go in the non-overlapped sections of the circles (1,2) and characteristics both systems share go in the overlapped section (3). Students could also try this comparing three economic systems.

• Have groups of students work to find out which countries have which type of economic system. Students can prepare their findings on a chart and use other visual aids.

• Although capitalism allows a lot of personal freedom and provides a high standard of living for many people, capitalist economics often face several problems (economic instability, inequalities in the distribution of wealth, neglect of the public interest). See if students can come up with any of these or other problems. Then, have pairs of students focus on one problem and ask people in the business world to cite examples of the problem. As a class, go over the examples and compile the information.

• Have students research to find out how capitalism, or one of the other types of economic systems, developed.

• Let students set up their own "class business" (i.e. bakery, car wash, pet-sitting, etc.). Students should decide who will be the investors and workers, who they want to sell to, how to market the product/service, how much to charge for it, what supplies need to be purchased, competition, etc. Let them really try it!

• Have each student write an essay giving his/her opinion of whether he/she thinks capitalism is the best economic system for our nation.

• Students can write stories pretending the U.S. has an economic system other than capitalism. It can be real or pretend. Students should include the type of economic system it is, details of it and how life is different with this system.

Notes/Ideas for Next Time

_____
_____
_____
_____
_____
_____
_____
_____
_____
_____
_____
_____
_____
_____
_____
_____
_____
_____
_____
_____
_____
_____
_____
_____
_____
_____
_____
_____
_____
_____
_____
_____

Consumer Choices

Economics

Name _____

Using newspapers and magazines, cut out two advertisements for similar products. Describe each one below. Include the price of each.

_____

_____

_____

_____

_____

_____

_____

Which item would you buy?

_____

Why was this your choice?

_____

_____

Staple the advertisements to the back of this paper.

Look through the papers or magazines again for an advertisement of a product you would like to promote more effectively. Staple the advertisement in the box. Write new copy for the product on the lines below.

_____

_____

_____

_____

_____

_____

_____

_____

_____

_____

Getting Started in a Business

Economics

Name _____

Every business begins with an idea or a need. Think of a product or service for which there is a need or of a product or service that needs improving and start a new business. Be creative.

What is your idea for a business? _____
_____

It will produce _____ a product _____ a service.

List the resources (land, labor, equipment, capital, management) you will need to start this business.

_____
_____
_____

List what you will need to spend money on to make your business successful.

_____
_____
_____

Draw a diagram to the right that shows the organization of workers in your business.

Answer the next three questions pretending that 1) your business is a single proprietorship, 2) a partnership or 3) a corporation.

1. Where would you get the money to start a single proprietorship? _____
   A partnership? _____
   A corporation? _____
2. Who will make decisions in a single proprietorship? _____
   In a partnership? _____
   In a corporation? _____
3. How will the profits be shared in a single proprietorship? _____
   In a partnership? _____
   In a corporation? _____

Cold War

Concepts

- Cold war is the term used to describe the struggle between the former Soviet Union and its Communist allies and the U.S. and its non-Communist democratic allies.
- A cold war is not an armed conflict.
- The U.S. and the former Soviet Union were involved in a cold war for more than 45 years.

Objectives

- To understand the difference between a cold war and an armed conflict
- To learn about conditions of the Cold War between the U.S. and the Soviet Union
- To recognize feelings associated with disagreements

Vocabulary

Berlin Wall, capitalism, cold war, compromise, Eastern bloc, imperialism, Iron Curtain, neutral country, Western bloc

Materials

current newspapers and magazines, one copy of page 12 per student

Background Information

Most historians believe the Cold War did not begin until after World War II, but relations between the U.S. and the former Soviet Union had been strained since 1917 when the Russian Revolution established a Communist government. After World War II, two sides emerged—the Western bloc led by the U.S. and the Eastern bloc led by the former Soviet Union. Some nations remained neutral.

It was difficult to settle disputes through compromise during the Cold War as each side thought it was right and the other side was wrong. Each side increased its military strength.

Although no armed conflicts between the two blocs occurred during the Cold War, it was a time characterized by distrust, suspicion and misunderstanding. There were times when conditions were so intense that it was feared a third world war would erupt.

Teaching Suggestions

- Discuss friendship with students. Ask them on what friendships are based. Ask if friends can disagree and discuss ways disagreements can be resolved between friends.
- Have students tell about disagreements they have had with friends or family and how they were resolved.
- Have a discussion similar to the ones described above using countries as your subject. Ask students why friendly relations between countries are important. Ask why countries may disagree. See if students think two countries can disagree and still be friendly. Discuss ways disagreements between countries can be resolved.
- Assign groups of students to quickly find and list situations that preceded the American Revolution, Civil War, World Wars I and II and the Persian Gulf War. As a class, discuss if there would have been alternate ways to settle these situations.
- Have students look through newspapers and/or magazines for articles about disputes between countries, states, neighbors, friends, etc. Discuss situations that brought about each disagreement and how each is being settled. Have each student write his/her solution to the dispute.
- Review the vocabulary words with students. Discuss each word's relationship to the Cold War between the U.S. and the former Soviet Union.
- Ask students what situations led to the Cold War between the East and West. (spread of communism, former U.S.S.R. thought U.S. was planning a third world war, Berlin blockade, etc.) Discuss the consequences.
- Ask students if they have ever had phone privileges removed or been grounded as punishment. Have them tell how it felt to be cut off from their friends.
- Have students pretend an "iron curtain" has just been instated to divide their community. (You may want to specifically define its location.) In groups, have students write about the changes this "curtain" will bring. Have them be specific.
- Ask students what they think the best way to solve a dispute is. Have students apply their answers to one of the wars in which the U.S. has been involved.
- There are many songs about peace and friendship. Have pairs of students choose a dispute currently going on between two classmates, two cities, two countries, etc. for which to find a "theme song." The song should advocate peace. Have each pair tell why it chose the song it did. Tell students they may rewrite parts of the song to make it more appropriate if necessary. Let students sing the songs.
- Distribute activity page 12, *What's a Tree Between Neighbors?* Discuss the situation depicted. Tell students that they are to finish the rest of the comic. Explain to them that they do not necessarily have to show what they think is right. After students have completed their comic, let students share them. Put them on a bulletin board or bind several together to make small booklets that students can browse through at their leisure to see the various ways students handled the situation.

Notes/Ideas for Next Time

_____
_____
_____
_____
_____
_____

Social Issues

What's a Tree Between Neighbors?

Name _____

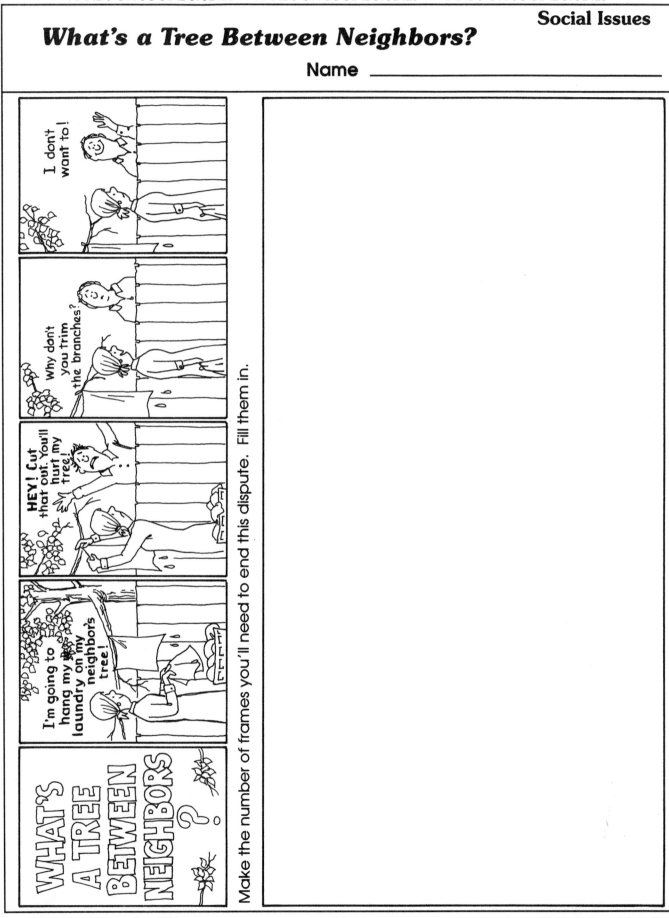

Make the number of frames you'll need to end this dispute. Fill them in.

Peace, a World Issue

Concepts

- Throughout history, people have wanted peace.
- There has seldom been a long period of peace in the world.
- Wars have been fought to achieve peace.
- Many people believe nonviolence is a better way to achieve peace.

Objectives

- To know that wars have been fought to solve many world disagreements
- To realize that one violent act usually leads to another
- To become aware of various nonviolent ways of ending conflicts

Materials

almanacs, encyclopedias, biographies of peacemakers, one copy of page 14 per student

Preparation

Save current news articles about conflicts and/or peace negotiations in the world. Cut out blue letters that read: "Symbols of Peace." Also cut out a white dove and a green olive branch. Attach them to a bulletin board lined with yellow paper. Ask your school librarian to collect biographies about peacemaking activists to put in a "peace library" under the "Symbols of Peace" bulletin board.

Background Information

There have been many attempts to keep world peace throughout history. In ancient times, the Olympic Games, held every four years, temporarily united the Greek city-states that were otherwise usually at war with one another. During the Middle Ages, the Christian church was the greatest force for peace. From the 1400's to the 1700's, many plans for lasting peace were made. A French educator, Baron Pierre de Coubertin, thought an international

sports competition would promote world peace, so he organized the modern Olympic Games which took place in 1896. After World War I, the League of Nations was formed, but it had little power and disbanded. In 1945, the United Nations was created. Its over 170-member nations work today for world peace.

Teaching Suggestions

- List some conflicts that have occurred throughout history. Discuss who was involved in each and the reason for the conflict. List the conflicts on a time line so students can see that there has seldom been a time since the beginning of civilization during which the entire world has been at peace. (Save this time line.) Ask students if these conflicts have resulted in a lasting peace.
- Share recent news articles about violent world conflicts with students. Discuss and locate where the problems are taking place, who is involved and why. (You could also assign students to do research on the cities/countries in conflict.) Ask students if they think the conflict(s) will be resolved through violence. What might they suggest as an alternative to violence?
- Explain to students that wars need not be fought in order to settle disagreements. Share articles with students about current peacemaking negotiations. Ask students if they think this is a better way. Let students give explanations for their reasons. You could also discuss the nonviolent ways of Ghandi, Martin Luther King, Jr., and Archbishop Desmond Tutu. The Camp David Accords are also a good example of nonviolent negotiations.
- Ask students what their first reaction is when someone hits them or calls them something unkind. Students will probably answer, "Strike back." Ask students what happens next. Does a fight solve the problem? Ask students what some better

ways are to solve a disagreement. Lead students in a discussion about nonviolence. Ask students if they think nonviolent techniques are effective. Have students give examples of how it is better to have a win/win situation (in which each side gets something), than a win/lose situation (in which one side is "put down"). Recall various disagreements at school involving students and how they were resolved.

- Look at the time line described in the first Teaching Suggestion. Ask students if they think those conflicts could have been resolved in a nonviolent way. Let them give examples.
- Explain to students that the dove and olive branch have been symbols of peace since ancient times when they represented good tidings. Instruct students to design a new symbol of peace and to write a paragraph explaining their choice. Put the new symbols up on the "Symbols of Peace" bulletin board.
- Have students write essays entitled either, "War—An Obsolete Solution" or "I Believe in War." Let students share them with the class.
- Cinquain, haiku, acrostic and rhyming are some types of poetry with which your students are probably familiar. Have students write and illustrate some type of poem depicting world peace. Share them with your class.
- Have students read a biography about a peacemaker and write a report on him/her.
- As you distribute activity page 14, *Peacemaker Award*, explain to students that Alfred Nobel, a Swedish chemist, felt guilty about all the destruction his invention of dynamite could produce. Because of this guilt, he established the Nobel Peace Prize which was first presented in 1901. It is given each year to a person who has furthered peace in the world. Tell students to read the directions on the activity page and to complete it independently.

Social Issues

Peacemaker Award

Name _____

Nominate a person whom you think is worthy of the "Peacemaker Award." He/she may be a world personality or one known only to you. Write about your person's peacemaking efforts and accomplishments.

_____ is my choice for the "Peacemaker Award."

_____

_____

_____

_____

_____

_____

_____

_____

_____

Fill in your recipient's certificate below. Describe your honoree by writing five sentences that begin with each letter of the word *peace*.

PEACEMAKER

Award

presented to

_____

P _____

E _____

A _____

C _____

E _____

14

Criminology

Social Issues

Concepts

- Crimes include a wide variety of misconducts forbidden by law.
- The degree of punishment for a crime varies according to its severity.

Objectives

- To understand that an offense, a misdemeanor and a felony are crimes of varying severity
- To understand that a crime is punishable by law

Vocabulary

abuse, assault, burglary, criminology, felony, larceny, misdemeanor, offense, premeditated, rehabilitation, robbery, vandalism,

Materials

one copy of page 16 per student

Preparation

Line a bulletin board with black paper. Cut out yellow letters that read: "POLICE BLOTTER." Attach them to the top center of the board. Cut three rectangles from yellow paper. Write one of the following on each one: Felony, Misdemeanor, Offense. These will be the headings of three columns under the title.

Background Information

Newspaper headlines and statistics too often indicate the rate at which serious crimes are committed in the U.S. Crimes may be classified according to their seriousness, for statistical purposes, according to the motives of the offenders, etc. Crimes are committed for various reasons. Criminologists examine factors related to crimes. People have long debated the kinds of punishments that should be carried out for crimes. Punishment serves to uphold the law and may deter some crimes.

Teaching Suggestions

- As an introduction, explain to students that criminology is a science. Ask them if they know what kind. (scientific study of crime, criminals and criminal behavior)
- Ask students what words they think of when they hear the word "crime." List their responses on the chalkboard. Add vocabulary words to the list if students' responses are light. Draw a line under the different kinds of crimes. Have students circle the crimes they believe are more violent.
- Write the three headings—Felony (serious crime), Misdemeanor (a lesser offense than a felony) and Offense (a crime)—on the chalkboard. Ask students to list the kinds of crimes that go under each.
- Have each student bring in a news article about a crime. Discuss the articles in class. Have students decide what type of crime each is. Put the articles on the "POLICE BLOTTER" bulletin board under the appropriate column.

  Have students follow any ongoing information about the crimes in the newspapers. Add additional articles to the board as each case develops. Students could also bring in written information about the crimes that they hear on the radio or TV.
- Discuss violence on TV with students. Have students watch a program on TV one night and list the violence in it (if any) on a sheet of paper. Discuss students' findings.
- Ask students if they can explain why crime has been on the rise and why they think many crimes are committed.
- Ask students for suggestions to deter crime. Ask them if they believe harsh punishments will stop criminals. Why or why not?
- Ask students if they think rehabilitation is a good idea for everyone. What ideas do they have for rehabilitation?
- Have students debate different kinds of punishments for crimes.

- Ask a law enforcement officer, criminal lawyer and/or judge to speak to your class. Have students prepare specific questions in advance.
- Have students make a chart comparing crime in your city/state/country to crime in other cities/states/countries. Why do some cities/states/countries have lower crime rates? Let students do research for the charts.
- Have students make a list of reasons why crimes are committed. Have them include ways to deter or stop crime, be it prevention or punishment.
- As you distribute activity page 16, *Famous Crimes*, tell students to follow the directions and complete it independently.

  After students complete the page, let them share some of their ideas. Then, tell them what actually happened. (Answers: Rosenbergs died in electric chair; Sacco and Vanzetti were executed; Hauptmann was executed.)

Notes/Ideas for Next Time

_____
_____
_____
_____
_____
_____
_____
_____
_____
_____
_____
_____
_____
_____
_____
_____
_____
_____
_____
_____

Famous Crimes

Social Issues

Name _____

Read about the three well known crimes below. On another sheet of paper, write what you think the punishment should have been for each one and why.

Rosenberg Spy Case

Julius and Ethel Rosenberg, husband and wife, were American citizens. Julius was fired in 1945 from the United States Army Signal Corps for being a Communist. Then, he worked with his wife's brother, David Greenglass, in a small machine shop they owned. Greenglass had previously worked on the atomic bomb project in 1944-1945 in Los Alamos, New Mexico. In 1950, Greenglass was arrested for spying while at Los Alamos, but he claimed his brother-in-law, Julius, asked him to collect the information. As a result, the Rosenbergs were arrested and accused of passing secret information about the atomic bomb to the Soviet Union.

Sacco and Vanzetti Case

Nicola Sacco was a shoemaker and Bartolomeo Vanzetti was a fish peddler. They were Italian immigrants who had come to America in search of better lives. In 1920, they were arrested and charged with the murders of two security guards. Both Sacco and Vanzetti were carrying pistols when they were arrested, and Sacco's gun was the same caliber that had been used to kill one of the guards. Because they supported anarchism, there was a lot of prejudice against these men. Anarchism is a philosophy which calls for the overthrow of all governments.

Lindbergh Kidnapping

Charles Lindbergh made the first solo nonstop flight across the Atlantic Ocean in 1927. Overnight, he became famous throughout the world. About five years later, his twenty-month-old son, Charles, Jr., was kidnapped. His dead body was found about ten weeks later. Several months after that, a carpenter, Bruno Hauptmann, was arrested and charged with kidnapping and murder. This kidnapping led Congress to pass the "Lindbergh law" which makes kidnapping a federal offense if the victim is taken across state lines.

Labor Movement

Concepts

- Management and labor have different goals.

Objectives

- To understand that unions want better working conditions and benefits for their members
- To understand that management wants to make money

Vocabulary

arbitrator, blue-collar workers, boycott, collective bargaining, craft union, grievance, guild, industrial union, mediation, open shop, picket line, right-to-work laws, scabs, strike, union security, white-collar workers

Preparation

Print a list of the vocabulary for each student. Write *labor* on enough small cards for half the class and write *management* on enough small cards for the other half of the class.

Arrange ahead of time to send half the class (labor group or management group) to the library while the other half remains in the classroom. (See explanation in Teaching Suggestions.)

Make a copy of page 18 for each student.

Background Information

The American labor movement refers to workers' collective efforts to improve their economic condition. Labor unions developed in the U.S. in the early 1800's when skilled workers in cities organized for higher pay. National trade unions began to develop during the mid-1800's, but none lasted very long. In 1881, Samuel Gompers organized a federation that included wage earners only. Eventually, the federation became known as the American Federation of Labor (AFL). Unions suffered setbacks over the next fifty years, but during the Depression, labor was preferred over big business. President Franklin Roosevelt passed several laws at this time which favored labor.

Workers in mass-production industries established the Congress for Industrial Organization (CIO). Its members included both skilled and unskilled workers. During World War II, labor leaders promised to back the war effort by not striking. However, after the war, there were major strikes because unions wanted their workers to get a fair share of America's new wealth. Then, automation and returning soldiers threatened the jobs of those who had stood by during the war. Several new groups of workers, including farmers and government workers, became unionized in the 1960's and 1970's. Currently, unions are on the decline. Union members have lost jobs as a result of foreign competition and a difficult economy.

Teaching Suggestions

- Give each student the vocabulary list. Instruct students to write the definition of each word as it pertains to the labor movement in America. They are not to use a dictionary for this activity. Discuss students' definitions when they have finished. Have them correct any definitions that they did not know or that were wrong.
- Ask students what labor unions do. (promote the welfare of wage earners by trying to improve their members' wages, hours, working conditions and job security) Write their responses and examples on the board. Ask students if they think unions are the best way to obtain benefits for workers. Ask why or why not.
- Discuss with students what management's goals are. Assign groups of students a profession. Have each group pretend it is the management of the assigned profession. Each group should make a list of its particular goals.

  Ask students what can happen when labor and management do not agree. Have each student give an example. It could be a local, national or international example.

- Tell students that they are going to negotiate a classroom contract. Divide them into two groups. Turn the labor and management cards you prepared upside-down on a table. Instruct each student to select a card. This will tell them to which group they belong.

  Establish ground rules. Tell students that the demands they make will pertain only to this class. The demands must be reasonable and such that they can be carried out within the classroom. Explain that you will be the recorder for both groups and that you also will have the right to disallow anything impracticable. (You know your group so guide them accordingly.)

  As a class, decide what issues should be considered in the contract (i.e. homework, discipline, seating, length of contract, etc.).

  Send the management group to the library as previously arranged. Instruct the labor group to decide specifically what "benefits" it wants for the students.

  Have labor present its demands to management. Send the labor group to the library. Have management consider labor's demands. It may agree to them or make an offer that meets some of the demands.

  Have management present its offer to labor. If an agreement cannot be reached, you will have to act as mediator and suggest solutions. If mediations fail, you will have to act as an arbitrator and make the decision for both sides.

  Tell labor and management that they are all students (workers) again. On the board, write the items settled upon in the negotiations. Hand out two copies of the *Classroom Contract* on page 18 to each student. Instruct students to fill in both contracts. When they are finished, students should sign both copies. Keep one and give one back to each student. A variation of this contract could be used in behavior modification cases or in a contract between the home and school or the home and student.

Labor Movement continued

Teaching . . . continued

- Have students write an essay giving their reasons why they would or would not join a labor union.
- See if someone from a local union can come speak to

students. Have students be prepared to ask questions.
- Let groups of students present situations in which labor has decided to strike. Let the rest of the class decide if they agree with labor or not. As a class, discuss solutions to the strike.

- Using an encyclopedia or other source, have students list as many labor unions in the U.S. as they can. Have them add any unions they think might be beneficial to certain groups of workers and tell why.

𝕮𝖑𝖆𝖘𝖘𝖗𝖔𝖔𝖒 𝕮𝖔𝖓𝖙𝖗𝖆𝖈𝖙

_____ , a member of the _____ class,
          (name)

enters into this contract with _____ . It is agreed that the first
                                    (teacher's name)

party will adhere to the rules set forth:

1. _____

   _____

2. _____

   _____

3. _____

   _____

4. _____

   _____

5. _____

   _____

This contract is valid from this day, _____ , at _____
                                        (month)   (day)   (year)   (time)

until _____ at _____ , at which time the contract ends.
        (month)   (day)   (year)   (time)

_____   _____
       (student's name)   (teacher's name)

_____   _____
          (date)   (date)

Gun Control

Concepts

- The Second Amendment to the Constitution is the basis of the gun control debate.
- The authors of the Second Amendment 200 years ago did not foresee how the use of guns would change.
- There are groups for and against gun control.

Objectives

- To interpret what the authors meant when they wrote the Second Amendment
- To interpret what the amendment could mean in today's world
- To recognize the two sides of the gun control debate

Vocabulary

assailant, automatic weapon, concealed weapon, handgun, militia, National Guard, National Rifle Association (NRA), Saturday Night Special, Second Amendment, semiautomatic weapon, Uzi

Preparation

Make enough copies of page 20 and of the Second Amendment for the class. (Or, write the amendment on the board.) For your convenience, the amendment is as follows: "A well-regulated militia, being necessary to the security of a free state, the right of the people to keep and bear arms shall not be infringed."

Background Information

The Second Amendment was written over 200 years ago. At this time, there was no standing army. Each state had its own militia in order to defend itself if necessary. State militias were made up of every able-bodied man in the state. When called to serve, each man had to bring his own gun.

Citizens who favor gun control may interpret the Second Amendment to mean that each state has a right to form a national guard and guns may be used for military purposes. Those who favor gun control believe individuals do not have the right to privately own guns.

Those who oppose gun control believe that the Second Amendment states that an individual does have the right to privately own a gun for purposes other than protecting the state. They claim the words "people" and "militia" mean Americans as individuals. They also contend that in the First and Fourth Amendments, "the right of the people" has always meant the right of the individual, so therefore, it should mean the same in the Second Amendment.

Teaching Suggestions

- Write the Second Amendment on the board or give each student a copy of it. Tell them that it was written over 200 years ago. Ask them what life was like then. Ask them what they think the authors meant when they wrote the amendment. Ask what it was the authors could not foresee.
- Tell students that the Second Amendment is the basis for the gun control debate today. There are groups like the National Rifle Association that lobby against any control. There are other groups who believe in strict gun control and others that believe in it but with some exceptions.
- Take a secret poll among your students. On a scrap piece of paper, have each student write his/her name and whether he/she is for or against gun control. Collect them. (The reason for a "secret" poll is so class members will not vote like their friends.)

  Tally the results. Then, ask students individually why they feel the way they do. Organize team debates on the issue.
- Distribute activity page 20, *A Case For or Against Gun Control.* Tell students to follow the directions and to complete the page independently.

- Assign groups of students different countries. Have each group research to find out as much information about guns in its assigned country as it can (i.e. gun control, number of people who own guns, number of deaths from guns each year, etc.). Instruct each group to compare its findings to the same information for the U.S.
- Invite a speaker who opposes gun control and one who favors gun control to come speak to the class.
- Have students make a list of real-life situations in which they wish there would have been gun control and in which they are glad there wasn't (i.e. assassinations of JFK, Martin Luther King, Jr., shooting of former President Ronald Reagan, etc.).

Notes/Ideas for Next Time

_____
_____
_____
_____
_____
_____
_____
_____
_____
_____
_____
_____
_____
_____
_____
_____
_____
_____
_____
_____
_____
_____
_____

A Case For or Against Gun Control

Social Issues

Name _____

Read each story below. Write a case for or against gun control after each story. Check which side you are taking for each one.

John, age 9, and Donald, age 14, were brothers. Donald got out of school earlier than John, so he was instructed to wait for John in front of school and walk home with him. Their parents worked, and the boys knew the routine they had to follow; first a snack, then homework, and then they could do whatever they wanted as long as they remained in the house or the yard. On one day in particular, the boys were examining their father's shotgun. They didn't know it was loaded. It accidentally went off and hit John in the shoulder.

_____ FOR _____ AGAINST

_____
_____
_____
_____
_____
_____

Late one Saturday night, a taxi driver picked up a couple that signaled for his service in front of a restaurant. They told the driver to take them to the riverfront. When the taxi turned into the park to cut across town, the man in the back seat held a knife to the driver's head. He told the driver to stop, to give him all the cash he had and to get out of the vehicle. The driver did as they ordered. Once out of the taxi, the man knocked the driver down and jumped into the front seat of the taxi. Just as the taxi was pulling away with the couple, the taxi driver pulled a gun from his pocket and shot at the tires of the cab. When the man got out of the taxi and came toward the driver with his knife, the driver shot the man.

_____ FOR _____ AGAINST

_____
_____
_____
_____
_____
_____
_____

20

Past, Present, Future

Making Predictions

Concepts

- Knowing the past helps predict the future.
- Changes are currently occurring faster in ten years than they used to in 100 years.

Objectives

- To learn some things about the past
- To be a risk-taker and predict the future

Vocabulary

extended family, forecast, nuclear family

Materials

wrapping paper, old sheets, dark crayons with wrappers removed, long strips of paper, brushes, books on transportation, chart paper, one copy of pages 23-26 per student

Preparation

Gather old photos and/or painting reproductions of scenes from 100 years ago, census records, old newspapers, etc. Send a letter (page 25) home to parents explaining the purpose of this unit, requesting that they share anything they might have that dates back 100 years ago or more. Make arrangements to visit a history museum and a cemetery. Make an activity sheet for students entitled *Cemetery Facts*. You will need to visit the cemetery ahead of time to learn what types of questions would be relevant for your class (i.e. Who is the oldest person in the cemetery? Who was the first to be buried there? Where else have you seen the family name, _____ , in our town? How many children did _____ have? etc.).

Background Information

Looking at the past helps predict the future. In order to understand how we arrived at the present, we need to know how things once were and how attitudes, trends and values have changed over a long period of time. There probably is no one who remembers life 100 years ago for you to talk to, but you can learn how people lived back then by visiting museums, looking at old pictures, going through old records and visiting cemeteries.

Change occurs much faster now than it did. For example, it took 100 years to go from the telegraph to the fax machine, from no concern about what we ate to high awareness of what not to eat, and from traveling short distances in a horse and buggy to orbiting Earth in a spaceship. In recent years, the compact disc has become the state-of-the-art format for listening to music, and people can live longer because of organ transplants.

Where are we headed in 2100?

Teaching Suggestions

- Ask students how they can find out about the past.
- Visit a history museum with the class. Tell the docent (if one is available, if not, you will have to familiarize yourself ahead of the visit) that you would like your class to "live" what life was like about 100 years ago. See if clothing, tools, furniture, entertainment, toys, utensils, etc., can be included.

  When you return from the museum, discuss with students what they saw and learned. Ask what some things were that they had never seen. Ask what (if anything) has replaced these things today. Discuss with students whether life at this time was easy or not.

- Visit a local cemetery. Take large wrapping paper or old sheets and crayons so students can make rubbings of the tombstones. Take the *Cemetery Facts* activity page you created and pencils. (Be sure to talk about acceptable cemetery behavior before arriving.)

  When you return, go over the *Cemetery Facts* activity page. Ask students what they learned about the past at the cemetery (life span, town fathers, family size, etc.). Hang up their rubbings.

Suggestions are given below for you and the students to use to explore the past involving family, work and travel. You will not want to do the following ideas all at one time. You may want to do these topics and/or different ones (i.e. education, architecture, communication, etc.).

Family

- Tell students that today they are going to talk about their families. If any student does not want to answer a question or contribute to the discussion, explain that that's okay, but the purpose of the activity is merely to establish a baseline. On chart paper, make a chart like the one shown. Begin the discussion by asking each student who lives in his/her house. (You

# living in household			
	S	N	E
father			
mother			
children			
other			

may want to explain nuclear and extended families before you begin. A nuclear family is a family unit with a father, mother and their children. An extended family consists of parents, children and other close relatives such as aunts or grandparents living in one household.)

After everyone who wanted to has answered, tally the results. Note the total number of families and the number that are single parent, nuclear and extended. Also tally the number of children per household.

Next, draw another chart as shown below. Draw it next to the one just completed. Ask students which adults in their family have a job outside the home. Tally their responses and then add up the results according to single parent, both parents and one parent in a nuclear family.

# work away from home			
	S	N	E
father			
mother			
children			
other			

Past, Present, Future continued

Making Predictions

Teaching . . . continued

- Distribute activity pages 23 and 24, *Family Statistics*. Explain to students that it is similar to the charts that were just made in class. Ask students to fill them in with an adult at home. Have students complete them as far back and for as many ancestors as they are able. Point out that on page 23, under mother's household, the student's mother's parents and the student's maternal grandparents should be written in. On page 24 under father's household, the student's father's parents and the student's paternal grandparents should be written in. Then, the next level is the student's great-grandparents. If they can go back further, tell them to make additional charts on the back of the page.

  Collect their findings. Make a composite of the facts: number of total families and number of single, nuclear and extended families and the average number of children per family at each level. Note if there is a trend in living conditions. Present the findings. Have students draw conclusions if any are to be drawn. Ask if they can think of any reasons for the changes.

Employment

- Look at pictures of people 100 years ago. Have students comment on what is happening, their appearance, etc.
- Ask students what kind of work their parents do. Make a chart similar to the one shown. Tally parents' occupations. Have students draw conclusions about the types of jobs held by their families. Keep the list for the record.

	Sales	Mfg.	Law	Medic
Father				
Mother				

- Distribute activity page 25, *Family Employment History*. Tell students to ask an adult at home to help them fill it out. When students have brought in the *Family Employment History* page, have students help you make a composite of them at each level and present them to the class. Ask students if they think the types of jobs have changed. If so, how? Why? What might this mean for future jobs?

Transportation

- Ask students how they came to school today. Ask if they think children 100 years ago came to school the same way. Why or why not? Ask students if they think students in the future will get to school the same way they do. If not, how? Let students illustrate their answers.
- Distribute copies of page 26, *Time Lines*. Tell students that they are to fill in the time lines with this year on the right and 100 years ago on the left. All dates go on top and the events go under the dates. The first time line should encompass the past 100 years of transportation. Let students use encyclopedias and other books you have gathered. For the other two time lines, let students work in groups. Each group can choose any two categories to research and depict over the last 100 years on the time lines. (Or, you may want to give each group two categories to research so groups won't research the same things.)

  When students have finished, have the groups paint the events of their time lines on butcher paper. Be sure students include dates and other information they want.
- Lead a discussion predicting the future 100 years from now using the same categories researched for the time lines. Ask students on what they base their predictions.

  Have the groups design and paint their predictions for one of their categories and add it to their time line.

Notes/Ideas for Next Time

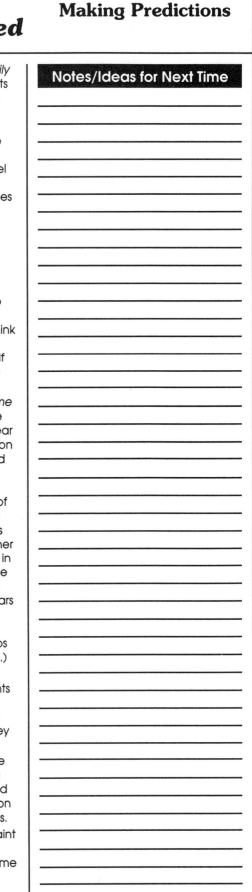

Family Statistics

Name _____

Student's Mother's Household

	# live in household			# work away from home		
	S	N	E	S	N	E
FATHER						
MOTHER						
CHILDREN						
OTHER						

Grandparents' Household

	# live in household			# work away from home		
	S	N	E	S	N	E
FATHER						
MOTHER						
CHILDREN						
OTHER						

Grandparents' Household

	# live in household			# work away from home		
	S	N	E	S	N	E
FATHER						
MOTHER						
CHILDREN						
OTHER						

Great Grandparents' Household

	# live in household			# work away from home		
	S	N	E	S	N	E
FATHER						
MOTHER						
CHILDREN						
OTHER						

Great Grandparents' Household

	# live in household			# work away from home		
	S	N	E	S	N	E
FATHER						
MOTHER						
CHILDREN						
OTHER						

Great Grandparents' Household

	# live in household			# work away from home		
	S	N	E	S	N	E
FATHER						
MOTHER						
CHILDREN						
OTHER						

Great Grandparents' Household

	# live in household			# work away from home		
	S	N	E	S	N	E
FATHER						
MOTHER						
CHILDREN						
OTHER						

Family Statistics continued

Making Predictions

Name _____

Student's Father's Household

	# live in household			# work away from home		
	S	N	E	S	N	E
FATHER						
MOTHER						
CHILDREN						
OTHER						

Grandparents' Household

	# live in household			# work away from home		
	S	N	E	S	N	E
FATHER						
MOTHER						
CHILDREN						
OTHER						

Grandparents' Household

	# live in household			# work away from home		
	S	N	E	S	N	E
FATHER						
MOTHER						
CHILDREN						
OTHER						

Great Grandparents' Household

	# live in household			# work away from home		
	S	N	E	S	N	E
FATHER						
MOTHER						
CHILDREN						
OTHER						

Great Grandparents' Household

	# live in household			# work away from home		
	S	N	E	S	N	E
FATHER						
MOTHER						
CHILDREN						
OTHER						

Great Grandparents' Household

	# live in household			# work away from home		
	S	N	E	S	N	E
FATHER						
MOTHER						
CHILDREN						
OTHER						

Great Grandparents' Household

	# live in household			# work away from home		
	S	N	E	S	N	E
FATHER						
MOTHER						
CHILDREN						
OTHER						

_____

Dear _____

We are studying the past (about 100 years ago) in order to predict the future. Your child will be asking for help in filling in family background information. We understand that you may not always have the answers or want to give them, but any help will be appreciated.

Also in our search into the past, we will be looking at old photos, pictures, diaries, letters, etc. that show and tell about life long ago. If you have anything you would care to share, I will see to it that it is well taken care of.

Thank you in advance for your cooperation.

_____

Family Employment History

Fill in the main work or employment of your ancestors.

Mother's Family Work Description	Father's Family Work Description
Grandfather _____	Grandfather _____
Grandmother _____	Grandmother _____
Great grandfather _____	Great grandfather _____
Great grandmother _____	Great grandmother _____
Great grandfather _____	Great grandfather _____
Great grandmother _____	Great grandmother _____
Great-great grandfather _____	Great-great grandfather _____
Great-great grandmother _____	Great-great grandmother _____
Great-great grandfather _____	Great-great grandfather _____
Great-great grandmother _____	Great-great grandmother _____
Great-great grandfather _____	Great-great grandfather _____
Great-great grandmother _____	Great-great grandmother _____
Great-great grandfather _____	Great-great grandfather _____
Great-great grandmother _____	Great-great grandmother _____

If you know anything about your great-great-great grandparents' employment, write it below.

_____   _____

_____   _____

_____   _____

_____   _____

Time Lines

Making Predictions

Name _____

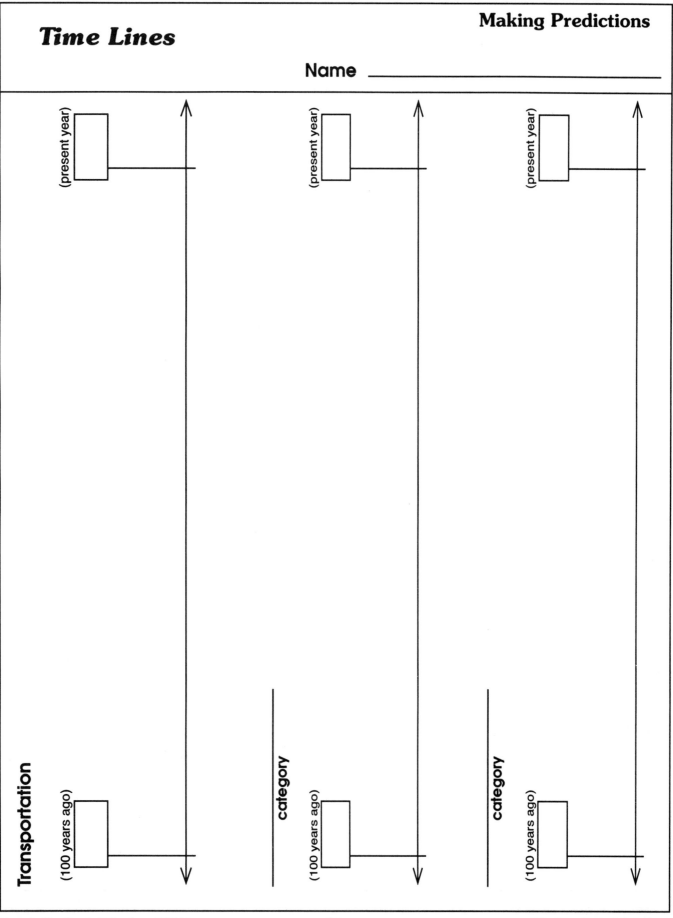

Transportation

(present year)

(present year)

category

(present year)

category

(100 years ago)

(100 years ago)

(100 years ago)

Language

Concepts

- Language is the most common form of communication.
- Language has made advanced civilization possible.
- There are many different languages.
- People who live together usually speak a common language.

Objectives

- To realize that language developed through a need to communicate
- To see that language transmits thoughts between people
- To realize that people who speak a common language can communicate
- To learn how to communicate without speaking

Vocabulary

etymology, idiom, jargon, linguistics, morphology, semantics, slang, syntax

Materials

apples, index cards, one copy of pages 28 and 29 per student

Preparation

Print the sentences below (or make up some of your own) on index cards.

(My) dog wags its tail. (A) big bell rang. See me run to the desk. (A) rabbit hopped (on) the (path). (The) eraser fell on the floor. Run and jump over the (stream).

Write charade ideas on index cards. (See Teaching Suggestions.)

Background Information

Language is the most common form of communication. It allows people to exchange thoughts and ideas. It can be written or spoken.

Wherever humans inhabit the Earth, there is language. According to linguists, there are about 6,000 languages spoken in the world today, but many of them are spoken by only small groups of people. At least 24 of them, however, have over 50 million speakers.

It is believed by scholars that language was probably a series of crude sounds in the beginning. It may have developed as the human brain and speech organs evolved. No one knows for sure. The first evidence of language is writing. Scholars believe that writing probably did not appear until thousands of years after spoken language originated. No one knows why languages change, but they do as long as they are spoken.

Teaching Suggestions

- Lead students in a discussion about language. Ask them why they think language began. Ask them how the first people communicated with one another and how they think language developed.
- Explain to students that you are going to try to speak to them without using your voice. You will try to impart a sentence. They are to tell you what you are communicating. Demonstrate "I love to eat apples." **I**—point to yourself; **love**—hug yourself or draw a heart in the air; **to eat apples**—pick up apples and pretend to eat.
  Pass out the sentence cards to students. Let them try to communicate the ideas on the cards. Explain to students that the words in parentheses may have varying responses. For extra fun, let students make up and act out their own sentences.
- Explain the game of charades to students. (There are several variations.) Tailor the rules for your students. Divide the class in half. Have students sit in two lines with their backs to each other. Instruct each group to number off—1, 2, 3, etc. Number One will be the first person to act out a charade. Number Two will follow and so on. Instruct Number One, or the actor of each group, to stand in front of his/her group. Tell the actors they should not look at the card you give them until you say "Go." Then, each actor should announce the category, hold up fingers to show how many words the answer contains and act it out. The first team to correctly guess each charade wins a point.
  You may want to demonstrate a charade category (i.e. Song—"The Star-Spangled Banner"). Talk it out as you do it so all students understand.
- Discuss the vocabulary with students. Have them give several examples of idioms, jargon and slang.
- Explain to students that there were words for things in the past that are seldom used now (i.e. icebox, teletype, etc.). Have students make a list of as many of these types of words as they can. (They may ask their parents or grandparents for help.) After comparing students' lists, discuss what new words replaced the old words and why.
- Have each student choose (or assign them) a foreign language. Have students research the language, the countries in which it is/was spoken, when it originated, etc. Have students prepare reports to present to the class. Encourage students to use visuals (maps statistics, etc.) in their reports.
- Explain to students what language families are. (groups of languages that are related because they all slowly developed from one earlier language known as the parent language) Different sources will identify different language families. Using encyclopedias and other sources, have groups of students research language families. On a large map of the world, each group should color in the areas where the languages in its language family are spoken. The groups could present all kinds of information on its language family.
- Distribute copies of activity pages 28 and 29, *Many Uses of Language*. Have students complete them independently.

Many Uses of Language

Communication

Name _____

An idiom is an expression that usually cannot be translated literally. Example: "It's raining cats and dogs." Never has it rained cats and dogs, but the idiom expresses how very hard it is raining.

Write your own idioms for the underlined words below.

The baseball player <u>ran quickly</u> around the bases. _____

The sun <u>suddenly set</u> and was not seen again until morning. _____

The <u>huge</u> insect flew against the screen. _____

The sudden blast made me <u>jump</u>. _____

He aggravates me <u>so much</u>. _____

My legs were <u>weak</u> after running the race. _____

It was <u>very dark</u> in the cellar. _____

The moonlight <u>was so bright</u> on the path. _____

The children <u>were impolite</u> in the assembly. _____

The vase <u>broke into many pieces</u> during the earthquake. _____

Select any group of people. The group may consist of family, friends, professionals such as doctors, lawyers, computer technicians, etc. Write a conversation they might have or a story about them using their "special" language or jargon.

Group Selected _____

_____

_____

_____

_____

_____

_____

_____

_____

_____

_____

_____

_____

_____

28

Many Uses of Language continued

Communication

Name _____

Some words have become obsolete, meaning they are not used any more. On the lines to the left, write some words we use today that may be obsolete in the future. On the lines to the right, write why they may become obsolete.

_____   _____
_____   _____
_____   _____
_____   _____
_____   _____

Computer, compact disc, laser, Jeep™, air conditioning and microwave are words that were not part of the English language 100 years ago. Explain why.

_____
_____
_____
_____

Invent a language of the future. On the lines below, write three nouns, verbs, adjectives and adverbs along with definitions for each.

Nouns/Definitions_____   **Adjectives/Definitions** _____
_____   _____
_____   _____
_____   _____

Verbs/Definitions _____   **Adverbs/Definitions**_____
_____   _____
_____   _____
_____   _____

On the back of this page, write three sentences using as many of the above words as you can. Use connecting words (prepositions, conjunctions, etc.) that you would normally use. Keep proper nouns the same.

Read your sentences out loud. They may sound peculiar, but it is possible that 1,000 years from now, a strange language will have replaced the English language as we know it today.

The Struggle for Equality

Human Rights

Concepts

- The involvement of African Americans in the civil rights movement began in the 1950's in America.
- Congress passed the Civil Rights Act separate from the Constitution.
- Not all civil rights acts are racially oriented.

Objectives

- To learn about African Americans' involvement in America's civil rights movement
- To know the contents of the Civil Rights Acts
- To realize that different groups demand civil rights for different reasons

Vocabulary

American Civil Liberties Union (ACLU), boycott, disabilities, Equal Employment Opportunity Commission (EEOC), freedom rides, National Association for the Advancement of Colored People (NAACP), quotas, segregation, sit-ins

Materials

copies of *Synopsis of Civil Rights Acts* (page 32)

Preparation

Make enough copies of activity page 32, *Synopsis of Civil Rights Acts*, and activity page 33, *Writing It Right!*, for every student.

Background Information

Civil rights are the rights every member of a community, state or nation has. They guarantee equal treatment for all people. Until the 1950's, however, states had laws that segregated races in public schools, recreational facilities, restaurants, hotels and train accommodations, restrooms and on buses. In other states, poll taxes kept African Americans from voting. Some states even enacted a "separate but equal" law in 1896, which guaranteed that, although they would be separate, the schools, places of recreation and other public facilities for African Americans would be just as good as the ones for whites. These practices showed disregard for a person's civil rights.

African American involvement in America's civil rights movement began in the mid-1950's. The Supreme Court overturned the separate but equal law after Thurgood Marshall's presentation of the *Brown v. Board of Education of Topeka* case in 1954. Rosa Parks' refusal to give up her seat to a white man on a Montgomery bus in 1955 further sparked the controversy and caught the attention of Martin Luther King, Jr. Against violence, King supported the boycott of the bus company that followed Parks' act. The bus segregation ordinance was declared unconstitutional following the boycott. In 1960, another important incident fueled the civil rights movement. A group of African American students refused to move from a lunch counter when they were denied service. By September of 1961, it was estimated that over 70,000 students, black and white, had participated in one of these sit-ins. These events and others propelled the African American cause in civil rights.

But not just African Americans have been discriminated against in our country. Many minority groups including women, Hispanics, Jews, immigrants, Native Americans and many others have often been, and unfortunately are still discriminated against. It is a goal of our country to end discrimination against these groups in areas like housing, education, employment and recreation and to guarantee equal rights and opportunities for all people.

Teaching Suggestions

- Ask students what kinds of rights they think are covered in the Civil Rights Acts.
- Explain to students that until the mid-1950's, the NAACP had been a very influential African American force behind the civil rights cause. In the '50's, names like Rosa Parks, Martin Luther King, Jr. and Thurgood Marshall began to emerge in the African American movement for civil rights. Discuss some specific events that involved these people and others. If students don't know anything about these events, provide materials they can use to learn about them.
- Ask students what boycotts, sit-ins, freedom rides and marches were. Ask what good they did. Have students explain the role these acts played in the struggle for civil rights. Discuss with students if they think these acts were more effective than violent ones. Have students write essays on violence vs. nonviolence as a means of achieving certain goals. Have them include people who support each view.
- Distribute copies of page 32, *Synopsis of Civil Rights Acts* time line, to students. Talk about each act in order. Discuss why each was needed and what it accomplished. Have students give examples of how they think each one worked.
- Have students listen as you read some of the situations below and on page 31. Students should tell you which act is being demonstrated or violated. After you have read each one, have each student come up with one to read to the class to let students figure out which act is being violated/demonstrated.
  —Virginia had not been allowed to vote before, so she got help registering. (1960)
  —The doors were open to everyone who wanted to see the movie. (1964)

The Struggle for Equality continued

Human Rights

Teaching . . . continued

—My father realized that the government was using an incorrect middle name for him. (1974)

- Divide the class into small groups. Assign one of the acts from page 32 to each group. Have students role-play a situation involving the act.

- Tell students they are to write three Class Rights Acts that they would like to see enacted. Have students include why they feel the acts are important. When they are complete, collect them. Group those that are similar and read them to the students. Have the class vote on those they want as Class Rights. Appoint students with good handwriting to rewrite the Class Rights Acts. Post them in the room.

- Assign each of a number of groups of students a minority group. Have the students research to find out how the groups have been discriminated against, what has been done to help them, etc. Let students present their information to each other.

- Have students write poems about discrimination, inequality, equality, etc. Students can share their poems with the class.

- Explain to students that a principle called due process requires the government to treat people fairly. Have students write and find examples of how our government does/does not follow this principle. Then, each student should compare our government's treatment of its people with the treatment people in another country receive from their government.

- Have students bring in newspaper articles dealing with civil rights and/or discrimination. Emphasize that the articles can relate to one or a group of people, our country or a different one, etc. Discuss the articles.

- Let students make a time line mural depicting the civil rights movement. Students can include drawings of famous people and events.

- Give each student a copy of activity page 33, *Writing It Right!* After students have completed the page, let them share their messages.

- From page 32, have students choose the Civil Rights Act they feel had the biggest impact on the largest number of people and tell why.

- Have students choose famous people or events dealing with discrimination and/or prejudice. Each student should prepare a report about the person or event and present it to the class.

- Each student should select and read a book dealing with discrimination. Have students prepare creative book reports using props, creative dramatics, etc. to tell others about their book. Make a list of all the books students read available so students have the opportunity to read more.

- Have each student write three math word problems using facts and figures from historical or current events involving discrimination. Compile them into a class book.

- Let groups of students make up short skits in which they include one or some of the following: sit-in, segregation, boycott, demonstration, march, violence, nonviolence, etc. The groups can perform for each other. Videotape if possible.

- Perhaps students feel that other acts or laws could be passed to help ensure equality for all people. Have pairs of students come up with at least one such act/law. Let the pairs present their acts/laws and reasons they feel they are necessary.

- Have students complete the following in a journal: "I am not prejudiced because . . . " "I have shown prejudice when I . . ."

Notes/Ideas for Next Time

Synopsis of Civil Rights Acts

Human Rights

Name _____

1957 — Civil Rights Act of 1957 set up the Commission on Civil Rights to investigate charges of denials of civil rights. It also created the Civil Rights Division in the Department of Justice aimed at enforcing federal civil rights laws and regulations.

1960 — Civil Rights Act of 1960 provided referees to help African Americans register to vote.

1964 — Civil Rights Act of 1964 was the strongest civil rights bill in U.S. history. It:
  • ordered businesses that serve people to do so without regard for race, color, religion or national origin.
  • barred discrimination by employers and unions.
  • established Equal Employment Opportunity Commission to enforce fair employment policies.
  • cut off federal funds from any program or activity which allowed racial discrimination.

Civilrite Realty
HOUSE FOR SALE

1968 — Civil Rights Act of 1968 ended discrimination in sale or rental of housing.

1974 — Privacy Act:
  • Made it possible for U.S. residents to check themselves in government files and request correction.

Right of Privacy Law:
  • How this law is interpreted depends on a person's interests:
    Recognized people's right not to have pictures used for advertising without permission.

Rita Love
MOVIE STAR
DRINKS
Slurp

1990 — Americans with Disabilities Act protected handicapped people from discrimination by private employers; required that buildings and mass transportation be accessible to disabled people; ordered phone companies to provide devices to people with speech and hearing disorders so that they can make and receive calls.

1991 — Civil Rights Act makes winning job discrimination suits easier for workers. Employer must prove that his/her hiring or promotion practices are necessary to his/her business. It gives victims the right to sue for monetary damages in cases of intentional job discrimination based on sex, religion, national origin or disability.

Writing It Right!

Name _____

If you could write one message to tell the world to end discrimination, what would it be? Write it in the sign above. On the lines below, write why you chose this message and why you think it would be the most effective.

_____

_____

_____

_____

_____

_____

_____

_____

_____

_____

_____

_____

33

Equality for All!

Human Rights

Concepts

- Every human is entitled to human rights.
- Some people have been deprived of human rights since the beginning of civilization.

Objectives

- To realize that nationality, race, religion, political beliefs, age and/or sex do not deny a person human rights
- To learn how to help people suffering from violations of their human rights
- To become aware of the abuse of human rights now and in the past

Vocabulary

atrocities, barbarous, bigotry, dignity, discrimination, genocide, inalienable, political prisoners, prejudice, racism, stereotype

Materials

The *Universal Declaration of Human Rights* (pages 35 and 36), one copy of page 37 per student, encyclopedias

Preparation

Make two copies of the *Universal Declaration of Human Rights*. Cut one into segments.

Obtain names of human rights organizations from the United Nations, Red Cross or your school or local library.

Have your school librarian collect books about human rights for your students to use with the acts described under Teaching Suggestions.

Background Information

Unfortunately, atrocities have occurred since the beginning of civilization. For example, millions of people have been murdered, imprisoned and/or kept as slaves because of ethnic group, political beliefs and/or race.

Every person is entitled to human rights. Human rights allow people to live freely with respect and dignity no matter who they are or what they believe. Human rights enable people to live free of torture and slavery. They provide all humans with the right to an education, food, shelter, clothing and medical care. These and other rights are listed in the *Universal Declaration of Human Rights* which was adopted and proclaimed by the United Nations on December 10, 1948. This declaration entitles all people to the rights it contains which are upheld by the United Nations.

Teaching Suggestions

- Go over the vocabulary with students. See if they can give examples as you discuss each word.
- Talk about stereotypical remarks and their appropriateness (i.e. Asians are good mathematicians, Germans are stubborn, etc.)
- Tell students about the *Universal Declaration of Human Rights*. Divide the class into small groups and assign segments of the declaration to each group. Going in the order presented in the declaration, have each group interpret its segment(s) and give a report on it to the class.
- Have students list human rights they feel they enjoy. Have them write a paragraph telling which right they feel is the most important.
- Ask students why they think some people have been deprived of their human rights in the past.
- Have students write a "Class Declaration." Have each student include three articles which he/she feels are the most important. Let students share their declarations and combine them to make the Class Declaration.
- Explain to students that human rights have been violated since the beginning of civilization. Have students look through a collection of books in the classroom or library

or in encyclopedias for information about a period of time in which human rights were violated and write a report. Some topics include: Crusades, holocaust, slavery, Native Americans, civil rights, apartheid, Ottoman Empire, Soviet Union, Ku Klux Klan, Iran, Iraq, Ethiopian famine, the war in Bosnia, and so on.

- Have students write a story using one of the story starters below or give them one of your own.
  They threw me into prison . . .
  There has been a drought for two years . . .
  Hundreds of us were crowded into one room . . .
  I could never leave . . .
- Ask students if they think human rights are being violated today. Have them look in magazines and newspapers for articles about the topic. Have students share any articles they find with the class. Have students hang the articles on a bulletin board.
- Give each student a copy of activity page 37, *Who Can Help?* Have students make up or write about a situation in which people's human rights have been violated. Students should fill in the information about who can or did help the situation and how.
- Ask students what they could do personally to help prevent or stop the deprivation of human rights. List their suggestions. Have them decide on one and plan a school/community project (i.e. walkathon, fund raiser, etc.).

Notes/Ideas for Next Time

_____
_____
_____
_____
_____
_____
_____
_____
_____

34

Universal Declaration of Human Rights

Preamble

Whereas recognition of the inherent dignity and of the equal and inalienable rights of all members of the human family is the foundation of freedom, justice and peace in the world,

Whereas disregard and contempt for human rights have resulted in barbarous acts which have outraged the conscience of mankind, and the advent of a world in which human beings shall enjoy freedom of speech and belief and freedom from fear and want has been proclaimed as the highest aspiration of the common people,

Whereas it is essential, if man is not to be compelled to have recourse, as a last resort, to rebellion against tyranny and oppression, that human rights should be protected by the rule of law,

Whereas it is essential to promote the development of friendly relations between nations,

Whereas the peoples of the United Nations have in the Charter reaffirmed their faith in fundamental human rights, in the dignity and worth of the human person and in the equal rights of men and women and have determined to promote social progress and better standards of life in larger freedom,

Whereas Member States have pledged themselves to achieve, in co-operation with the United Nations, the promotion of universal respect for and observance of human rights and fundamental freedoms,

Whereas a common understanding of these rights and freedoms is of the greatest importance for the full realization of this pledge,

Now, Therefore, **The General Assembly** proclaims **This Universal Declaration of Human Rights** as a common standard of achievement for all peoples and all nations, to the end that every individual and every organ of society, keeping this Declaration constantly in mind, shall strive by teaching and education to promote respect for these rights and freedoms and by progressive measures, national and international, to secure their universal and effective recognition and observance, both among the peoples of Member States themselves and among the peoples of territories under their jurisdiction.

Article 1

All human beings are born free and equal in dignity and rights. They are endowed with reason and conscience and should act towards one another in a spirit of brotherhood.

Article 2

Everyone is entitled to all the rights and freedoms set forth in this Declaration, without distinction of any kind, such as race, colour, sex, language, religion, political or other opinion, national or social origin, property, birth or other status.

Furthermore, no distinction shall be made on the basis of the political, jurisdictional or international status of the country or territory to which a person belongs, whether it be independent, trust, non-selfgoverning or under any other limitation of sovereignty.

Article 3

Everyone has the right to life, liberty and security of person.

Article 4

No one shall be held in slavery or servitude; slavery and the slave trade shall be prohibited in all their forms.

Article 5

No one shall be subjected to torture or to cruel, inhuman or degrading treatment or punishment.

Article 6

Everyone has the right to recognition everywhere as a person before the law.

Article 7

All are equal before the law and are entitled without any discrimination to equal protection of the law. All are entitled to equal protection against any discrimination in violation of this Declaration and against any incitement to such discrimination.

Article 8

Everyone has the right to an effective remedy by the competent national tribunals for acts violating the fundamental rights granted him by the constitution or by law.

Article 9

No one shall be subjected to arbitrary arrest, detention or exile.

Article 10

Everyone is entitled in full equality to a fair and public hearing by an independent and impartial tribunal, in the determination of his rights and obligations and of any criminal charge against him.

Article 11

(1) Everyone charged with a penal offence has the right to be presumed innocent until proved guilty according to law in a public trial at which he has had all the guarantees necessary for his defence.

(2) No one shall be held guilty of any penal offence on account of any act or omission which did not constitute a penal offence, under national or international law, at the time when it was committed. Nor shall a heavier penalty be imposed than the one that was applicable at the time the penal offence was committed.

Article 12

No one shall be subjected to arbitrary interference with his privacy, family, home or correspondence, nor to attacks upon his honour and reputation. Everyone has the right to the protection of the law against such interference or attacks.

Article 13

(1) Everyone has the right to freedom of movement and residence within the borders of each State.

(2) Everyone has the right to leave any country, including his own, and to return to his country.

Article 14

(1) Everyone has the right to seek and to enjoy in other countries asylum from persecution.

(2) This right may not be invoked in case of prosecutions genuinely arising from non-political crimes or acts contrary to the purposes and principles of the United Nations.

Article 15

(1) Everyone has the right to a nationality.

(2) No one shall be arbitrarily deprived of his nationality nor denied the right to change his nationality.

Article 16

(1) Men and women of full age, without any limitation due to race, nationality or religion, have the right to marry and to found a family. They are entitled to equal rights as to marriage, during marriage and at its dissolution.

(2) Marriage shall be entered into only with the free and full consent of the intending spouses.

(3) The family is the natural and fundamental group unit of society and is entitled to protection by society and the State.

Article 17

(1) Everyone has the right to own property alone as well as in association with others.

(2) No one shall be arbitrarily deprived of his property.

Article 18

Everyone has the right to freedom of thought, conscience and religion; this right includes freedom to change his religion or belief, and freedom, either alone or in community with others and in public or private, to manifest his religion or belief in teaching, practice, worship and observance.

Article 19

Everyone has the right to freedom of opinion and expression; this right includes freedom to hold opinions without interference and to seek, receive and impart information and ideas through any media and regardless of frontiers.

Article 20

(1) Everyone has the right to freedom of peaceful assembly and association.

(2) No one may be compelled to belong to an association.

Article 21

(1) Everyone has the right to take part in the government of his country, directly or through freely chosen representatives.

(2) Everyone has the right of equal access to public service in his country.

(3) The will of the people shall be the basis of the authority of government; this will shall be expressed in periodic and genuine elections which shall be by universal and equal suffrage and shall be held by secret vote or by equivalent free voting procedures.

Article 22

Everyone, as a member of society, has the right to social security and is entitled to realization, through national effort and international co-operation and in accordance with the organization and resources of each State, of the economic, social and cultural rights indispensable for his dignity and the free development of his personality.

Article 23

(1) Everyone has the right to work, to free choice of employment, to just and favourable conditions of work and to protection against unemployment.

(2) Everyone, without any discrimination, has the right to equal pay for equal work.

(3) Everyone who works has the right to just and favourable remuneration ensuring for himself and his family an existence worthy of human dignity, and supplemented, if necessary, by other means of social protection.

(4) Everyone has the right to form and to join trade unions for the protection of his interests.

Article 24

Everyone has the right to rest and leisure, including reasonable limitation of working hours and periodic holidays with pay.

Article 25

(1) Everyone has the right to a standard of living adequate for the health and well-being of himself and of his family, including food, clothing, housing and medical care and necessary social services, and the right to security in the event of unemployment, sickness, disability, widowhood, old age or other lack of livelihood in circumstances beyond his control.

(2) Motherhood and childhood are entitled to special care and assistance. All children, whether born in or out of wedlock, shall enjoy the same social protection.

Article 26

(1) Everyone has the right to education. Education shall be free, at least in the elementary and fundamental stages. Elementary education shall be compulsory. Technical and professional education shall be made generally available and higher education shall be equally accessible to all on the basis of merit.

(2) Education shall be directed to the full development of the human personality and to the strengthening of respect for human rights and fundamental freedoms. It shall promote understanding, tolerance and friendship among all nations, racial or religious groups, and shall further the activities of the United Nations for the maintenance of peace.

(3) Parents have a prior right to choose the kind of education that shall be given to their children.

Article 27

(1) Everyone has the right to freely participate in the cultural life of the community, to enjoy the arts and to share in scientific advancement and its benefits.

(2) Everyone has the right to protection of the moral and material interests resulting from any scientific, literary or artistic production of which he is the author.

Article 28

Everyone is entitled to a social and international order in which the rights and freedoms set forth in this Declaration can be fully realized.

Article 29

(1) Everyone has duties to the community in which alone the free and full development of his personality is possible.

(2) In the exercise of his rights and freedoms, everyone shall be subject only to such limitations as are determined by law solely for the purpose of securing due recognition and respect for the rights and freedoms of others and of meeting the just requirements of morality, public order and the general welfare in a democratic society.

(3) These rights and freedoms may in no case be exercised contrary to the purposes and principles of the United Nations.

Article 30

Nothing in this Declaration may be interpreted as implying for any State, group or person any right to engage in any activity or to perform any act aimed at the destruction of any of the rights and freedoms set forth herein.

Who Can Help?

Human Rights

Name _____

Many organizations—local, national and international—uphold people's human rights. The United Nations, individual governments, non-government human rights groups and even individuals can work to protect human rights.

Find or make up a situation in which human rights have been violated. Then, find out who can/did help remedy the situation. Write what they can do or did do to help.

Green Acres
PUBLIC
Country Club
AND
Golf Course
FOR MEN ONLY

Internationally— _____

_____

_____

_____

_____

Nationally— _____

_____

_____

_____

_____

Human Rights Groups— _____

_____

_____

_____

_____

Individuals— _____

_____

_____

_____

_____

Me— _____

_____

_____

_____

_____

Taking the Census

U.S. Constitution

Concepts

- Every ten years, a census is taken in the U.S.
- The U.S. census is taken in every year that ends in zero.
- The U.S. census tells who the people are as a nation at a given time.
- U.S. population information and figures change every ten years.

Objectives

- To understand why the U.S. takes a census every ten years
- To understand what kind of information is needed in a census
- To gather information
- To draw conclusions from combined data

Vocabulary

census, decennial, enumeration, apportionment, data, statistics, categories on *Census Form* (page 39)

Materials

official state manual/handbook, almanacs

Preparation

Make enough copies of the following for every student:
1) *Required by Law* (page 39);
2) State census statistics from an official state manual/handbook.

Background Information

Article I, Section 2 of the U.S. Constitution states that a national census must be taken every ten years. Among other things, this information helps determine the number of representatives each state sends to Congress. The first census was taken in 1790. Every person who lives within the U.S. borders as of April of the year the census is taken is supposed to be counted in the decennial census. Information about the people counted is also gathered so that our country's needs can be determined.

Teaching Suggestions

- Begin by distributing a part of Article I, Section 2 from the U.S. Constitution (*Required by Law*, page 39). Discuss the meaning of the underlined words. Establish what the census is, why and when it is taken, etc. Explain how the representation of each state in Congress is based on population. Ask students if they think this is fair. Why or why not? Ask them why they think the writers of the Constitution wrote this as they did. If the first census was taken in 1790, have students figure out how many censuses have been taken in the U.S. Ask them when the next census will be taken.

  Option: The rest of the reproduced section of the Constitution (other than the underlined words) may be interpreted with the class, though much of it has changed.

  Discuss with students the kind of information, other than population figures, that a census can provide: number of males/females, number of children per family, growth of racial and ethnic groups, number of males/females who work, education, people's ages, growth in certain areas of our country, movement of people, etc. Have each student choose three categories and list ways for each that the government could use this information. Then, have students list other groups or organizations that could use this information and how they could use it.

- Share with students the census facts about your state. (These can be found in an official state manual/handbook.) Reproduce current and past figures. Compare them. Ask students if the number of representatives in your state has changed. See if students know how many representatives your state has in Congress and who the representative from your district is. Compare your state's representation in Congress with

other states. (Use an almanac.) Let students decide if your state is small, medium or large according to population figures.

- Have students use state and national population figures and information to write math word problems. Compile them into a class book and have students work them.

- Have students come up with some census questions that could help give the government a current picture of certain situations in our country and that could also help the government plan for the future.

- Distribute the bottom of activity page 39, *Census Form*. Go over it with the class. Be sure students understand what is called for (i.e. race—African American, Caucasian, etc.). Instruct students to ask a parent or guardian the questions on the *Census Form*. Emphasize that only one person in the household is to answer the questions. Have students bring the completed form back to class. On an opaque projector, record the answers from the *Census Form*. Have students calculate averages to get a picture of your classroom population where applicable. From that, have students draw some conclusions. For instance, would a builder want to build apartment buildings in the area, or could the homes in the area soon be in need of repairs?, etc.

  For more practice and fun, expand this activity by asking another group (i.e. grandparents, friends, etc.) the same or different questions. Students could include a variety of questions to find out all kinds of information.

- Call a "town meeting." Invite your district's representative to speak to your students about the size, make-up and requirements of the district. Invite your students' families and other community members to attend. Have all students prepare a question they would like to ask the representative. Collect them and select the most appropriate ones.

U.S. Constitution

Required by Law

Name _____

Part of Article I, Section 2 of the U.S. Constitution reads as follows:

". . . Representatives and direct taxes shall be apportioned among the several States which may be included within this Union, according to their respective numbers, (which shall be determined by adding to the whole number of free persons, including those bound to service for a term of years, and excluding Indians not taxed, three-fifths of all other persons). The actual enumeration shall be made within three years after the first meeting of the Congress of the United States, and within every subsequent term of ten years, in such manner as they shall by law direct. . . ."

Census Form

Name of person answering questionnaire _____

Address _____
      #   street   city   state   country

Where born _____ If not U.S., when came to U.S. _____

Age _____ U.S. citizen yes _____ no _____

Race _____ Sex _____ Marital Status _____

Years of school: Elem_____ J.H.S._____ H.S._____ Coll._____ Grad_____ Other_____

Total number of people living in household _____

Name	Age	Where Born	Race	Sex	Marital Status	U.S. Citizen	Business

If more space is needed, write on the back of this paper.

Type of Housing:

single dwelling _____   apartment _____   condominium _____   mobile home _____

unit shared with business _____   other _____

Do you own? _____   rent? _____   other? _____

age of home _____

Civil Rights

Concepts

- Civil rights allow every person to receive fair and equal treatment.
- Civil rights are mentioned in the main body of the U.S. Constitution, but it is in the Bill of Rights and in certain amendments that much consideration is given to them.
- All civil rights have limits. For example, civil rights cannot be used to justify actions that could harm the safety, health, welfare or morals of others.

Objectives

- To understand what a person's civil rights are
- To recognize the presence of civil rights in the Constitution and in the amendments
- To recognize that civil rights have limits

Vocabulary

bill of attainder, capitation, discrimination, due process, ex post facto, habeas corpus, poll tax

Materials

copies of the Preamble, Articles I, III, IV and the amendments to the U.S. Constitution, one copy of page 42 per student

Preparation

Make enough copies of the Preamble, Articles I, III, IV and the amendments to U.S. Constitution for every student.

Background Information

All people have the right to be treated equally and fairly. People's rights and civil rights are synonymous including the freedoms of speech, assembly, religion, press, trial by jury, choice, etc. When the U.S. Constitution was first written, people's rights were mentioned in the main body of the document, but many people believed they did not go far enough. In order for the Constitution to be ratified, the Bill of Rights had to be added to it. Other amendments, some considering people's rights, have been added over the years as necessary.

Teaching Suggestions

As part of the activities presented deal with the Constitution and part deal with the amendments, you may want to do the activities in two sections.

Section One

- Go over vocabulary with students.
- Ask students the meaning of civil rights and what they think some civil rights are.
- Distribute copies of the Preamble and Articles I, III and IV of the Constitution. Have a student read the Preamble aloud while others follow. Ask students if they believe that the Constitution intends for everyone to be treated fairly. Ask them which words verify their opinion.
- Have students write a new, more modern Preamble to the Constitution. It should have the same meaning as the original.
- Have students read through Article I to find the parts that protect a person's civil rights. (Section 9) Discuss what rights are protected. Ask students why they think *habeas corpus* is important enough to be in the Constitution. See if students can tell you how an ex post facto law protects a person's rights.
- Have students read through Article III to find parts that protect a person's civil rights. (Section 2) Discuss the right protected (trial by jury) and why it is guaranteed. Let students hold a mock trial in your classroom. They can "try" a student(s) for a crime involving civil rights.
- Read the following (taken from Article I, Section 9) to the students: "No capitation, (or other direct) tax shall be laid, unless in proportion to the census . . ." Ask students what those words mean. Ask students if they think a poll tax is fair and why or why not. Then, explain to students that the 16th Amendment authorized Congress to pass an income tax law. See how much students know about income tax. Then, let each student choose a career and decide how much money he/she makes. (Students should be realistic.) Have them find out the federal income tax rate and the income tax rate for your state. Students should next figure out what they have to pay in federal and state income tax each paycheck. Ask students why some states do not have an income tax.
- Instruct students to look through Article I for other evidences of discrimination (Section 2, (2) ". . . three-fifths of all other persons.)" and Section 9, (1)". . . ten dollars for each person.") Discuss how they violate a person's rights. Have groups of students make lists of people who they feel are discriminated against today and how. Students could bring in newspaper or magazine articles defending their views.
- Have students read through Article IV for evidence of discrimination (Section 2, (3) ". . . No person held to labor or service . . ."). Discuss it. Point out the use of the word "citizen" in Section 2, (1). Remind students that slaves were not considered citizens. Have students pretend they are slaves. Have them write about the country they came from and include details about it (i.e. location, climate, geographical features, etc.).
- Have students add a new article to the Constitution dealing with civil rights and relating to problems facing our society today. Have students share them with the class.

Section Two

- As you distribute the amendments to the Constitution, explain to students that several states would not ratify the Constitution without a Bill of Rights to protect the rights of the people. A promise was

Civil Rights continued

U.S. Constitution

Teaching . . . continued

made that it would be done, and so the first action of the new Congress was to write a Bill of Rights. The first ten amendments to the Constitution are called the Bill of Rights. The other amendments have been added as necessary over time.

- Go through the amendments in order. Have a student read each one aloud. As a class, decide which ones are intended to protect people's rights and which rights they protect. After discussing how these amendments protect people's rights, ask students if these amendments have any exceptions or limitations.

- Have each student choose one amendment he/she thinks is the most important. Have the students write it at the top of a piece of paper and under it write why they feel it is the most important.

- Let students decide which, if any, amendments need to be deleted or changed. Have them give reasons for the deletions or changes.

- Have students read through the amendments and write down all the ones which pertain to civil rights.

- Using newspaper and magazine articles, have students bring in articles relating to one of the amendments. Let students share them with the class.

- An amendment mural would be fun for your students or groups of students to make. Students could cut out or draw pictures and words pertaining to the amendments and display them on an "Amendment Mural."

- Some amendments have been added to repeal or change other amendments. Have students make a list of these.

- Have students compare amendments to the U.S. Constitution with any

amendments to your state constitution. Are any similar?

- Have students write civil rights poems. They can be acrostic, haiku, rhyming or other types of poetry dealing with civil rights. Let students illustrate them.

- Instruct students to research and write about any historical event involving civil rights. Make a time line on which students can write the date of the event after they share it with the class.

- Present the situations below to students. Ask them if any rights are being violated. If so, have them tell you which right and who is being violated. (Feel free to add situations of your own.)

—Mary's house was searched from top to bottom for evidence by police without a search warrant. (Amendment 4)

—Sam did not rent his apartment to the couple who answered his ad because of their religion. (Amendment I)

—Two people were hurt in the rush to evacuate the theater after Janice falsely yelled "FIRE." (Amendment I)

—Michael was excited when he turned 18 because that meant he could vote in the upcoming Presidential election. However, because he looked so young, he was told he could not vote. (Amendment 26)

—A crowd gathered around Stanley as he stood on a homemade platform in Town Park yelling obscenities and untruths about the city's government and urging all to join him in taking over city hall. (Amendment 1)

- Let students present situations similar to those listed above. Lead a discussion on whether there is a need for any more amendments and what they might be.

- As you distribute activity page 42, Next?, explain to the class that there almost was a 27th Amendment known as the Equal Rights Amendment, or the ERA. However, only 35 states had

ratified it when the deadline ran out. It needed the ratification of 38 states. Have students complete the activity page independently.

Notes/Ideas for Next Time

_____
_____
_____
_____
_____
_____
_____
_____
_____
_____
_____
_____
_____
_____
_____
_____
_____
_____
_____
_____
_____
_____
_____
_____
_____
_____
_____
_____
_____
_____
_____

U.S. Constitution

Next?

Name _____

#27

The Equal Rights Amendment (ERA) reads:
"Equality of rights under the law shall not be denied or abridged by the United States or any state on account of sex."

Equality for WOMEN

What did it mean to accomplish? _____
_____

Give an example. _____
_____
_____

Do you think it should have been ratified? Why or why not? _____
_____
_____
_____

On another sheet of paper, write a letter to one of your representatives or senators in Washington, D.C., and give him/her your opinion of the Equal Rights Amendment.

#28

Write a 28th Amendment you feel is necessary. _____
_____
_____

Give an example of a situation it would avoid. _____
_____
_____

On posterboard, make a sign in favor of your proposed amendment. Show it to your class. Present your amendment and argument for it to your classmates. Have them vote on it. If $^2/_3$'s approve it, you win!

28th Amendment
The right to shop at malls shall not be denied on account of age.

State Government

Concepts

- Every state has a constitution.
- A state government may take an action that does not conflict with the powers delegated to the U.S. by the Constitution.
- State and local governments have some autonomy.

Objectives

- To learn about state governments
- To understand that there are limits to the laws a state may pass
- To recognize different levels of government
- To learn to compare different types of government

Vocabulary

autonomous, jurisdiction, revoke

Materials

state manual or handbook, opaque projector, state constitution, U.S. Constitution, a copy of page 45, *Some Are Legal, Some Are Not*, for each student

Preparation

Write to the office of your state's secretary of state for copies of your state constitution, a state manual/handbook and any other information they might have about your state government.

Make enough copies of your state constitution for every other student.

Make enough copies of the U.S. Constitution for every other student.

Divide your state constitution into parts (i.e. articles or sections of articles, bill of rights or individual rights, etc.). You will need one part per student, pairs of students or groups of students. Write each part on a separate sheet of paper.

Background Information

Although it is one of 50, your state is unique. Its size, shape, symbols, demography, industry, system of government, etc., set it apart from all the others. Even though all states share some similarities with other states as outlined in the U.S. Constitution, each state retains its autonomy at the same time.

Teaching Suggestions

You will probably want to divide this section into at least three class sessions not including visitors or the field trip.

- Ask students if they know of any laws that pertain to the governing of their community.
- Ask students why they think it is necessary to establish laws about how a community is governed.
- Ask students to find out what kind of document (if any) there is that establishes the laws for their community.
- Ask students what document establishes the federal government and its duties. (U.S. Constitution)
- With the class, look at copies of the U.S. Constitution. Based on the background knowledge of your class, review whatever parts of the Constitution you feel are necessary. Pay particular attention to Article I, Section 10, Article IV and Amendment 10. (If your class has not studied the Constitution, go over each part in depth so students understand its structure and the powers it gives the federal and state governments.) Ask students the questions below about what states can and cannot do as established in the Constitution.

(1) Why isn't it a good idea for states to make their own money?
(2) What else are states not allowed to do?
(3) What might happen if states were allowed to have a king/queen?
(4) Do you think it's a good idea that states not have a permanent army?
(5) What could happen if states had treaties with each other?
(6) Do you believe states should respect each other's laws? Explain your feelings.

(7) What might happen if one state could make an agreement with another?
(8) If you moved to another state, would you be treated differently from its citizens? Explain your answer.
(9) What does the U.S. guarantee every state? (1. a republican form of government in which the people elect representatives to govern; 2. protection against invasion and domestic violence)
(10) Why do you think the Tenth Amendment was added to the Bill of Rights?

Let students choose any of the above questions about which to write an essay or make up a story. (For example, students could pretend two states made an agreement and write about it.)

- Distribute copies of your state constitution to students. (Or, put one up on an opaque projector if you are not able to get enough copies.) Do the same with the U.S. Constitution.

Begin by giving the students some information about your state constitution (i.e. when it was originally written; if it was ever rewritten, etc.). Establish when the U.S. Constitution was written. Discuss its revisions. What provision was made to keep it up-to-date?

- Go over your state constitution unit by unit with students. Establish which general topics both the U.S. Constitution and your state constitution have in common (i.e. Executive, Legislative, Judicial, etc.). When students are aware of which topics are the same, ask them some of the questions below and on page 44 or make up some of your own.

(1) Who is in the executive branch? Are they all elected, appointed or members of the same political party? How long are their terms? Who is the governor? Who is the lieutenant governor or equivalent?

State Government *continued*

Teaching . . . continued

(2) How is the state legislature set up? How many members does it have? How is this number determined? How long are members' terms? Are there any requirements for being a state legislator?

(3) Describe the state judicial system. How does it differ from the federal court system?

(4) Does the state constitution have a bill of rights? Where is it located? How many rights does it list? Whom do they protect? Are any the same as in the U.S. Constitution? Are any different than the U.S. Constitution?

(5) What provision is made for amending and/or rewriting the state constitution?

(6) What is covered in your state constitution that is not in the U.S. Constitution? What is covered in the U.S. Constitution and not in your state's?

Once you have discussed this information with the class, have students work in groups to compare their state government with the federal government. One group could compare the Executive Branch, one the Legislative Branch, etc. Let the groups present their comparisons using charts.

• Give each student a slip of paper with the name of a part (i.e. article, section, bill of rights, just one right, etc.) of your state constitution written on it. You may give every student a different part or you can give two to three students, who will work together, the same part. Tell students that they are to study the part of their state constitution written on the paper and report about its content and meaning to the class. Have them compare it to the U.S. Constitution if applicable.

• Tell students to look in the paper for articles about the state legislature or issues confronting the state. Have them bring the articles in to share with the class.

Hang the articles on a bulletin board. Have students follow the stories if they are ongoing.

• Have students find out who represents them in their state legislature and have them write a letter to their representative(s) 1) inviting him/her to speak to the class, 2) suggesting a need for some action, 3) asking how he/she voted or is going to vote on an issue, or 4) offering support or criticism for a representative's performance.

• If feasible, take students on a field trip to your state capital. Let them observe the legislature at work. Write to your representatives ahead of time. Ask them to meet with the students. Perhaps arrange to meet the governor.

• Invite a local official (mayor, judge, etc.) to talk to the class. Have the official be sure to point out his/her ties to federal and/or state government and the autonomy of his/her duties.

• Share a state handbook/manual with the class. Discuss the kind of information it contains (government, history, geography, places of interest, important people, sports, highways, etc.). You could also do a whole class project researching these various topics on your state. Let groups of students choose a topic to research and present to the class.

• Distribute activity page 45, *Some Are Legal, Some Are Not.* Explain to students that several simulated laws will be described. Some could pass. Others could not. The students are to indicate whether the law could or could not pass as described and write the reason for his/her choice.

• Ask students what kinds of services their state provides (education, public safety, public works, recreation, health, welfare, conservation, agriculture, and business and labor). Divide students into nine groups. Have each group research one of these areas and provide as much information for it as they can

(i.e. newspaper articles, organizations, programs, activities, etc.).

• Have groups of students compare their state constitution with another state's constitution. How are they different? Why are they different? Let students present their findings to the class.

• Assign students different countries to find out if they are broken up into political units like states. If so, how do they compare to our states?

Notes/Ideas for Next Time

_____
_____
_____
_____
_____
_____
_____
_____
_____
_____
_____
_____
_____
_____
_____
_____
_____
_____
_____
_____
_____
_____
_____
_____
_____
_____
_____
_____

Some Are Legal, Some Are Not

State Constitutions

Name _____

Write if each situation below could be legal or not.
Then, explain the reason for your choice.

1. The U.S. Congress passed a law stating that any state that so wishes can make its own money.

   ____ could be legal   ____ could not be legal

   _____

   _____

   _____

   _____

2. Congress declared war on a foreign country after the country refused to stop shooting at visiting Americans.

   ____ could be legal   ____ could not be legal

   _____

   _____

   _____

3. The state legislature passed a law agreeing to trade with any country.

   ____ could be legal   ____ could not be legal

   _____

   _____

   _____

4. The U.S. Congress established the salaries for the governors of the states.

   ____ could be legal   ____ could not be legal

   _____

   _____

   _____

5. The state legislature set the date for electing a new governor.

   ____ could be legal   ____ could not be legal

   _____

   _____

   _____

Immigration

Concepts

- America is a nation of immigrants.
- Assimilation into a new culture can be difficult.
- The number of immigrants allowed in the U.S. each year is restricted.
- Immigrants have made the U.S. a richer nation.

Objectives

- To understand that many families originally came from outside the U.S.
- To recognize that immigrants may have problems adjusting to a new culture
- To understand the reasons for immigration quotas
- To understand that immigrants have enriched America's culture
- To understand that immigrants to the U.S. have sometimes been perceived as a threat to people already in America

Vocabulary

alien, ancestor, assimilation, deportation, descendant, emigration, ethnic, generation, ghetto, heritage, naturalization, passengers, prejudice, quota, refugee, steerage, visa

Materials

markers, bleached muslin or old sheeting

Preparation

- Cut material to flag size. Hem it where necessary.
- Make enough copies of page 48, *Family Chart*, so that each student gets two.
- Make one copy of page 49 per student.

Background Information

The U.S. has received more immigrants than any other country. For this reason, the U.S. is sometimes called the Nation of Immigrants. During colonial times, about one million people immigrated to America. Most came from England. These people brought their language and traditions with them which formed the basis for America's culture. By the time America claimed its independence from England in 1776, however, about two-fifths of its people were from countries other than England.

During the first 100 years of U.S. history, there were no immigration laws. At first, only about 10,000 immigrants came each year. After 1830, however, the number increased every ten years from 600,000 in the 1830's to 2,600,000 in the 1850's. From 1860 to 1890, more than ten million immigrants poured into the U.S. They came mostly from western and northern Europe. From 1890 to 1930, over 22,000,000 immigrants came to live in America. Most were from Greece, Hungary, Italy, Poland, Portugal, Russia and Spain.

The new settlers came for better job opportunities, good farmland and religious and political freedom. Those already here felt threatened by the great numbers of immigrants. They resented the newcomers and demanded that the government restrict their number. The first immigration law was passed in 1882. A law in 1917 made adult immigrants show that they could read and write at least one language. It also barred immigration from most of Asia and the Pacific Islands. In 1921 and 1924, additional laws were passed reducing the number of immigrants allowed to enter the U.S. However, after World War II, the immigration laws were eased.

Teaching Suggestions

- Ask students what they know about their roots (i.e. where their family came from and when). Let students see their heritage for themselves. Give them two copies of the *Family Chart* on page 48. Have them write "MOTHER" in the box at the top of one page and "FATHER" on the other page. Tell them to fill in the chart at home with the help of a parent. Instruct them to write the city and state or city and country in which each person was born on the line below his/her name. When students reach the first person born outside the U.S. on each arm, they should write the year of his/her arrival in the U.S. Tell students that they don't have to go any further on an arm of the chart once the year of arrival is filled in. When the charts are completed, have students bring them to class.

  When all the charts have been completed, ask students if anyone's entire family (all four arms) comes from only one country. Also, ask when these ancestors came to America. Then, ask students from what countries multiple ancestry families came and when. Point out that America is often called the Nation of Immigrants. Explain to students that some families might be called "Family of Immigrants." Ask students why.

  For extra fun, have students make a graph depicting the countries and years ancestors came to America.

- Ask students why immigrants come to America. Ask if they think new immigrants (including ancestors) had an easy time when they arrived in the new country. Lead the discussion with questions such as: "Did they know anyone already here? Was finding a job, a place to live, language, etc., a problem?" Continue by asking students if they think newcomers were always welcomed in the U.S. Why or why not? If necessary, lead students in a discussion saying, "When America built the railroad, workers from China were brought to America. What effect could this have had on the American worker?" Have students pretend they are immigrants in a new country. Have them write about their experience using factual details.

Immigration continued

Teaching . . . continued

- Ask students in what ways immigrants have enriched our country. Ask if there is any evidence in their community.

- Invite any person(s) from your area to speak to the class about the country from which they came, why they came, if assimilation was easy, etc. Perhaps a group of folk dancers might perform and teach the class traditional dances from their country.

- Ask students if they can name countries from which recent immigrants have come and why. Have students look in the newspapers for articles about current immigration practices. Speak about immigration quotas and lead students into thinking about the necessity of them.

- Distribute activity page 49, *Immigration Restrictions*, and have students complete it. (Answers to bottom of page: John Astor—A German-born fur trader and capitalist; He invested heavily in Manhattan Island farmland, which became part of New York City. Irving Berlin—A Russian immigrant; He composed many popular American songs including "White Christmas" and "God Bless America." Andrew Carnegie—Born in Scotland; He was a leading steel manufacturer and philanthropist. He donated much of his fortune to various cultural and educational causes such as the establishment of public libraries. Walter Gropius—A German architect; He helped spread the theories of modern European architecture throughout the U.S. as chairman of the Department of Architecture at Harvard University. Meyer Guggenheim—A Swiss-born financier and industrialist; His family donated much of his wealth to charitable causes including the Guggenheim Museum in New York City. Joseph Pulitzer—Hungarian-born; He was one of America's leading newspaper publishers and established the Pulitzer Prizes for achievement in journalism, literature, music and art. David Sarnoff—Born in Russia; He headed the Radio Corporation of America (RCA) in the 1930's and 1940's. He was one of the first people to see the full possibilities of using radio and television to entertain the public.)

- Have each student write a report on a famous U.S. immigrant.

- Divide your class into groups of four or five. (Group students according to the countries their families came from.) Have students make a flag of the country from which their ancestors came. Have them research reasons why people came along with customs, language, dress and food of the country. Students can report their findings to the class in a creative manner (dramatizations, dress, cooking, charts, diorama, etc.).

- Using an old sheet or bleached muslin and markers, have students make a flag representing all of the places students' families have come from.

- Have a Foreign Family Festival. Have each student dress in the clothes typical of the country from which his/her ancestors came. Have each student bring in a story, recipe, food, poem, song, etc., which represents the country and share it with the class. For more fun, do this activity with another class.

- Holidays are different all over the world. Have students research to find out what kinds of holidays are celebrated in the countries from which their ancestors came. Students can then make a large classroom calendar and write in the names of the holidays. Celebrate as many of them as you can.

- On a large map of the world, have students write their names in the countries from which their ancestors came. Have students research to find out about various geographical features the countries of origin contain.

- Students could write about these on index cards and run string from the index cards (attached around map) to the location of the features on the map.

- Set your class up with pen pals from a different country. Write to the address below to get more information. Your students will have lots of fun corresponding with students from a different country and will learn lots of information too.

  International Pen Friends
  P.O. Box 290065
  Brooklyn, NY 11229

- Have students pretend a group of 1,000 immigrants is coming to your city/town. Students should write what they would do to help acclimate these people to your city/town. What could students tell/show them to make their transition easier?

- Tell students to pretend that they have to immigrate to another country. Students should write why they are leaving and where they are going. They should include experiences once they get to the new country.

- Have groups of students list as many foods, songs, dances, books, movies, names, etc. as they can that Americans have borrowed/inherited from other countries.

- Have groups of students make a chart listing advantages and disadvantages of having immigrants come to the U.S. Compare the groups' charts.

Notes/Ideas for Next Time

_____
_____
_____
_____
_____
_____
_____
_____
_____
_____

FAMILY CHART

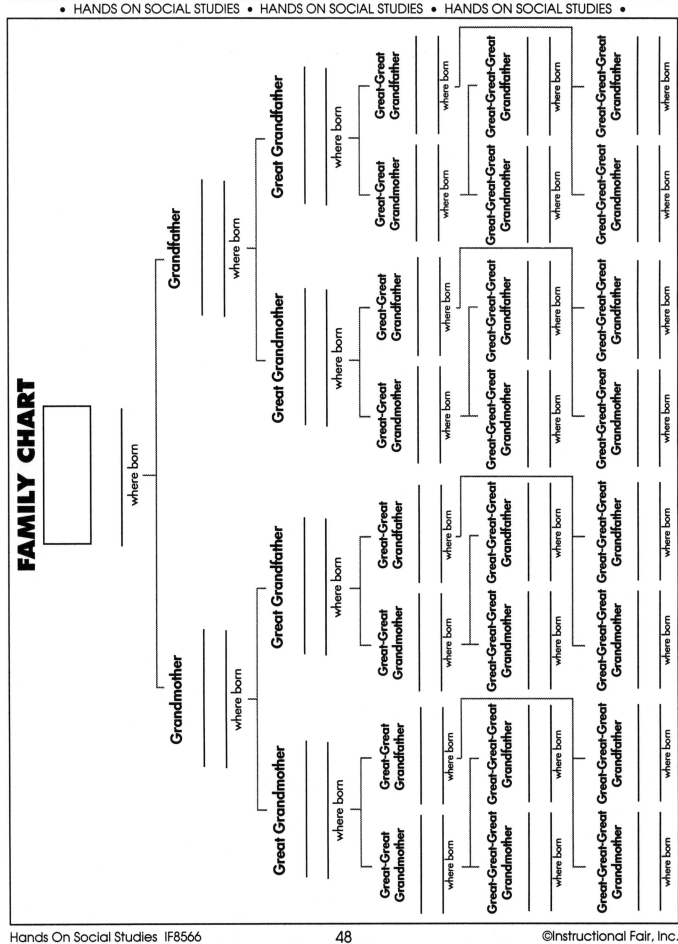

Immigration Restrictions

United States Law

Name _____

Often there is controversy concerning immigrants and their entrance into the U.S. Respond to the following statements by expressing your opinions about immigrants and immigration.

List standards you believe immigrants must comply with in order to gain entry into the U.S.

_____

_____

_____

_____

List reasons you think are valid to deny an immigrant entry into the U.S.

_____

_____

_____

Express your opinion about immigration laws and/or quotas. Should they exist?

_____

_____

_____

_____

Describe what the U.S. would be like if, after the colonists declared their independence from England, no more immigrants had been allowed to enter the U.S.

_____

_____

_____

_____

What might America have missed had the immigrants listed below not been allowed to enter the U.S?

John Astor _____

Irving Berlin_____

Andrew Carnegie _____

Walter Gropius _____

Meyer Guggenheim _____

Joseph Pulitzer _____

David Sarnoff _____

Political Parties

Concepts

- There are one-party and two-party systems.
- A voter has no choices in a one-party system.
- Political parties in a two-party system generally have a platform.
- Third parties develop in the U.S. when a large number of people want policies that the two major parties do not offer.

Objectives

- To learn the difference between a one-party and two-party system
- To understand what a platform is
- To understand why third parties develop
- To be able to defend an opinion

Vocabulary

platform

Materials

two card sets (described below), candy, one copy of pages 50 and 51 per student

Preparation

Make a set of cards equal to the number of students you have. Write "Communist" on each card. Make a second set of cards of equal number. On this set, write "Democrat" or "Republican" dividing the set so that you have three more Republican than Democrat cards. If possible, obtain the platforms of the Democratic and Republican parties from the national headquarters of your state.

Background Information

The U.S. Constitution does not mention political parties. Many of the Constitution's authors were opposed to them, but the Federalist and Democratic-Republican parties developed soon after George Washington became President. Many people believe the Democratic Party today originated from the Democratic-Republican Party. It is the oldest existing political party in the U.S. The Republican Party came into existence in 1854. It started as a series of antislavery political meetings.

The U.S. is a two-party system, but it also has or has had several third parties. None of the third parties has ever won the presidency, but the two major parties have had to adopt some of the third-party proposals because there was a lot of public support for them.

Teaching Suggestions

- Lay the Communist cards you prepared upside-down on a flat surface. Have every student take one. Tell students not to let anyone see their card, and that it contains the name of the party they belong to for this activity. Draw a chart like the one shown.

Party	Communist	Republican	Democrat
Candidate	No Recess	Candy	Pretzels

Tell students to raise their hands to vote for the "candidate" (Candidates include: 1. No recess, 2. Candy and 3. Pretzels) named on the party's ticket when you say it. Say "No recess." All students should raise their hands since they are all "Communists."

Notice students' reactions. Ask them what seemed to have happened. Explain that this is what happens when there is a one-party system. Ask students which countries have such a system. Ask students if they would want to live under such rule.

Have students throw away the Communist cards and take another card from the second set. Again, tell them not to let anyone see their card.

- Tell students again to raise their hands to vote for their party's "candidate" when you say it. Say "Candy." Write the number of votes it received next to it. Next, say "Pretzels." Write the number of votes it received next to it. Since "Candy" won, hand out a piece of candy to each student.

Ask students what the difference is between this vote and the last one. (one-party vs. two-party system) If students have no background knowledge about the Democratic and Republican parties, see that they get it now. Ask them what functions the parties have, what part they play in the government, and what their platforms are. Ask students what the two major U.S. parties are and why there is a need for more than one party.

- Explain to students that sometimes neither party satisfies a large number of voters. Therefore, a third party is formed. There have been several third parties in U.S. history (i.e. Liberal Republicans—1872, Roosevelt Progressives—1912, Gold Democrats—1896, Dixiecrats—1948, Greenback Party—1870's, etc.). Talk about some of them and their goals. Ask if a party concerned with one goal would have as good a party platform as a party with several goals. Ask students to explain why they believe as they do.

- Distribute activity pages 51 and 52, *Party Talk*, to students. Explain that students may join either major U.S. party, an existing third party, or create one of their own. Tell them to write their choice and then write the platform for that party. After they have established their party's platform, they are to take a position for or against the policies that follow and write a "speech" supporting that position. For extra fun, have students with opposing views debate the topics on the activity page.

- Divide students into three groups. Assign one group to be Republicans, one to be Democrats and one to be a third party. Have each group come up with an issue to debate. Let all groups prepare arguments for the situations and debate.

- Have each student choose a country and write about its political party(ies) system. Students should share the information with the class.

Party Talk

Name _____

Learn what the philosophies of the two major U.S. parties are. If you do not like the philosophy of either one, create a third party of your own.

Join one of the parties or make up your own. Name of the party to which you now belong:

_____

Write its philosophy or platform.

_____

_____

_____

_____

_____

_____

_____

_____

As a member of that party, take a position for or against the policies below. Write a "speech" supporting your opinion.

Some people want to limit the number of terms legislators may serve in Congress.

_____

_____

_____

_____

_____

_____

Many people believe all hunting of wild animals should be prohibited.

_____

_____

_____

_____

_____

_____

Party Talk continued

Politics

Name _____

Some propose to launch a permanent space station manned with ten astronauts for six months at a time.

_____

_____

_____

_____

_____

_____

Some hope to establish federal work programs so no one will remain unemployed for more than two months.

_____

_____

_____

_____

_____

_____

_____

Many people want dental care provided for every working American.

_____

_____

_____

_____

_____

_____

HELP KEEP OUR
AIR CLEAN

BAN
SMOKING

Select an issue or policy that is currently under consideration for becoming law. Write what it is. _____

_____

_____

Take a position for or against it and write a speech supporting your opinion on the back of this page.

Where Are We?

Concepts

- Maps and globes are printed representations of Earth.
- Imaginary lines of the surface of the Earth are called meridians (lines of longitude) and parallels (lines of latitude).
- Meridians extend from the North Pole to the South Pole and are at their greatest distance from one another at the equator.
- World time and locations are measured east and west of the Greenwich Meridian.
- Latitude describes the position of a point on Earth's surface in relation to the equator.
- Earth can be divided into four hemispheres.

Objectives

- To recognize Earth pictured on a flat or round surface
- To learn to locate places on a map, given longitude and latitude
- To learn to calculate time around the world, given the time at a specific longitude
- To be aware of Earth's four hemispheres
- To follow directions

Vocabulary

cartography, hemisphere, latitude, longitude, meridian, parallel

Materials

globe, world map, U.S. map, book of constellations, posterboard, two oranges or grapefruits, markers for bingo, strips of paper, stapler, crayons

Preparation

Cut posterboard into 5" squares. Make enough copies of *Measuring Mania* (page 55) and *Bingo Card* (page 56) for every student. Cut enough 2" x 18" white strips of paper for every student.

Background Information

With events occurring throughout the world as they are today, we can no longer be satisfied with knowing only about the location of our neighborhoods and cities. It is essential to know the location of places in the world to better understand history-in-the-making and the effect different events might have on various parts of the world.

Teaching Suggestions

Divide this unit into as many sections as are practical for your class.

- Have eight students stand in a circle. Holding hands, have them step back as far as they can to make as large a circle as possible. Next, tell them to drop their hands. Tell students to take one normal step forward and stop. Ask if they notice anything different about their position. Have students continue taking one step forward three or four more times until it is obvious that they are getting closer together. Have students sit down.

  Now, present students with a globe. Ask if they see any similarities between what they just did and something on the globe. Guide them if necessary to realize that they got closer together like the lines of longitude.

  Explain to students that when they started on the stretched-out circle, it was as if they were on the equator. Ask a student to point to the equator on the globe. Explain to students that the equator is the starting point for the degrees of latitude. These degrees measure distance from the equator to the poles. The latitude of the equator is zero. The North Pole has a latitude of 90° north (+90°). The South Pole has a latitude of 90° south (–90°). Continue explaining that on a globe, the equator is also the line on which equal distances are marked. These distances show degrees of longitude which measure east and west distances.

- Give each student a copy of activity page 55, *Measuring Mania*, to help them better understand longitude and latitude. When students have finished writing their own word problems, gather the problems together and put them into a booklet. Let students work the problems.

- Ask a student to run his/her finger along a meridian on the globe and on the map. Have the student tell in which direction the meridians travel (north/south) and where they seem to end. Conclude that they terminate at either pole and are closer together there.

- Have groups of students list ways globes and maps are alike and different. Compare students' findings.

- Ask students if there are other lines on the map. Ask them what they are and in which direction they travel. (lines of latitude—east/west)

  Ask students if these lines meet at a certain point like the meridians. Have students explain using the globe and map.

- Ask students what the 0° latitude is. (equator) Ask a student to point to it. Then, have a student point to different degrees of latitude. Ask where the parallels of latitude are in relation to the equator. Explain that they are noted by + (north) or – (south) to indicate north or south of the equator plus their number of degrees. Or, they are noted by their number of degrees followed by N or S. (Example: –45° = 45° S)

- Ask students how many degrees of latitude there are. (180°) Ask students where the largest number of degrees are located. (North and South poles) Ask students in which direction the lines of latitude go around Earth. (east/west)

- Ask students what information can be determined from longitude and latitude.

Where Are We? continued

Mapping

Teaching . . . continued

- Ask a student to point to the zero degree meridian. Tell them this is also called the prime meridian, or the Greenwich Meridian, because it runs through Greenwich, England. Any meridian west of it is usually noted with a W (i.e. 15° W). Any meridian to its east is often noted with an E (i.e. 90° E). World time is calculated from this meridian.

- Point out to the students that when it is noon in Greenwich, it is one hour earlier each longitude line to the west, and one hour later each longitude line to the east. Ask students to take turns pointing to different meridians in which the time would be 11:00 a.m., 6:00 p.m., etc., as you designate them compared to noon in Greenwich. Also, have students name some places that would have the same time along the designated meridian.

  Then, reverse this activity. Tell students to pretend that it is 2:00 a.m. in Greenwich. Then, ask them what time it would be in Los Angeles, Berlin, Sydney, etc.

  Further, ask students what meridian they are located on or are to the west of. Then, ask them what time it is in Greenwich now.

- Point out the International Date Line. Tell students that anything east of it is yesterday and anything west of it is today.

  Then, give every student a 2" x 18" strip of paper. Instruct them to 1) fold it into 3 equal sections, 2) fold it in half again to make 6 equal sections, 3) fold it in half again to make 12, and 4) fold it in half one more time to make 24 sections.

  Next, tell students to unfold the strip and draw a line on each crease. Students should now count in from the left (west) 12 lines and hold their finger on the twelfth line while they count from the right (east) 12 lines to make sure they land on the same spot. Once they are sure they have found the middle line, tell them to write noon across it and to go over the line with crayon

to indicate it as the Greenwich Meridian. Present students with the following: "If it is noon in Greenwich, what time is it on the next meridian to the west." Continue going all the way until the west "end" is reached. Have students write the times across each crease or line (11:00 a.m., 10 a.m., etc.).

Then, repeat this process traveling to the east. Let students see how it is midnight today and yesterday at the same time. Have them draw a line with a crayon on each end of the strip to show the International Date Line.

Have students staple the ends of the strip together to make a "24-hour time wheel."

- Briefly look at a map of the U.S. Ask students to determine on about which longitude they live. Remove the map. Tell students that for homework, they are going to find out what their latitude is. (Assign this activity when a clear night is forecast.) Tell students that they are not to look at a map. Rather, they are to find the North Star. It is the end star in the handle of the Little Dipper. Show students a picture of it in a book about constellations. Tell students that once they find the North Star, they should point to it with one arm. With the other arm, students should point to the horizon. (See diagram below.) Next, students should have a parent, sibling, friend, etc., measure the angle between their arms. This should roughly be the latitude where they are located.

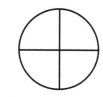

Students can check their findings against the map. Have students combine the latitude of their location with their longitude locale. Ask a student to write this location on the board (i.e. 38° N, 105° W) as everyone's "address."

- Give students specific places to find on a map. Have students estimate their approximate

"addresses" using latitude and longitude measurements.

- Take an orange or a grapefruit. Tell students to think of it as Earth. Draw a line around its fattest part and tell students that this is the equator. Ask students which direction is above the equator (north) and which is below it (south). Cut the fruit in half. Tell students that everything above the equator is in the Northern Hemisphere. Ask students where everything below the equator is located. (Southern Hemisphere) Ask students what a hemisphere is.

- Take another orange or grapefruit. Draw a line from the top to the bottom and around back up to the top. Tell students that one line is the Greenwich Meridian and the other line is the International Date Line. Cut the fruit in half. Ask students what each half is called. (Eastern Hemisphere, Western Hemisphere)

- Draw the diagram below on the board. Ask students to explain the two crossed lines and how it is possible to live in two hemispheres. Then, ask if they know in which two hemispheres they live.

- Ask students to put two fingers at different points on the same line (i.e. –15°, 60° W and +30°, 60° W or +45°, 105° W and +45°, 95° E). Ask students how the two points are alike and different.

- Give each student a copy of the blank *Bingo Card* on page 56. Have students fill in the spaces on the cards with letters which stand for two hemispheres in each quadrant of Earth (NE, NW, SE, SW). When their cards are ready, call off different places in the world—countries, rivers, cities, etc. Students will put a marker for each place on a square that names the two hemispheres in which it is located.

Mapping

Measuring Mania

Name _____

To better understand lines of latitude and longitude, meridians, the equator and much more, solve the story problems below.

1. Any point on Earth's surface completes a whole circle (360°) once every 24 hours. This happens because Earth turns on its axis once every 24 hours. How many degrees pass beneath the sun each hour? _____ Therefore, one hour of time equals _____ degrees of longitude.

2. Each degree of longitude is divided into 60 parts called minutes (written as 60'). Each minute is divided into 60 seconds of longitude (written as 60"). These minutes and seconds of longitude do not measure time. They measure distance. Fill in the chart below with the correct times.

   If 24 hours of time = 360° of longitude,

   then 1 hour of time = _____° of longitude,

   4 minutes of time = _____° of longitude,

   1 minute of time = _____' (minutes) of longitude

   and 1 second of time = _____" (seconds) of longitude.

3. Latitude and longitude are the two coordinates that locate any point on Earth. The latitude of a point is measured along an imaginary north-south line called a meridian. If the equator has a latitude of 0°, and the North and South poles have latitudes of 90°, how many degrees of latitude are there? _____

4. All points on the surface of Earth that have the same latitude lie on an imaginary circle called a parallel of latitude. List three other places which have the same latitude as your city/town. _____

   _____

5. The distance between two parallels of latitude that are about 1° apart is about 60 nautical (sea or air) miles or 69 land miles (111 km). Using this information, make up your own word problem. _____

   _____

6. Write three more math word problems on the lines below and on the back of this page using the information above.

   _____

   _____

55

Bingo Card

Mapping

Name _____

Write one of the underlined abbreviations that follow in each box. The letters stand for the hemispheres in parentheses after them. Write <u>NE</u> (northern and eastern), <u>NW</u> (northern and western), <u>SE</u> (southern and eastern) and <u>SW</u> (southern and western) in any order. You do not have to have an equal number of each.

That's Write!

Concepts

- Writing is a way of expressing a language through visual symbols.
- The first forms of "writing," or marking on objects, date back to the time of the earliest human beings.
- There are different alphabets used throughout the world.
- Writing is used for keeping records, informing, entertaining and influencing.

Objectives

- To understand that writing is an expression of language
- To understand that there are different alphabets in the world
- To understand why writing is necessary
- To understand that the first fully developed systems of word writing appeared about 5,000 years ago

Vocabulary

cuneiform, hieroglyphics, ideography, phonetic alphabet, pictograph, rebus, Rosetta Stone, rune

Materials

nails (one per student), candle stubs or fat crayons (one per student), dull knife, rolling pin, clay, posterboard, one copy of page 58 per student

Preparation

Write several alphabets (or perhaps an art teacher could write them for you). Make some large enough to put on a bulletin board entitled "Awesome Alphabets." On a large sheet of paper, write several more alphabets (i.e. ancient alphabets, Russian, Hindi, Hebrew, Arabic, Gaelic). Put Roman alphabet letters under symbols that represent the same letter/sound. Reproduce enough for every student.

Background Information

Writing is a system of human communication using visual symbols. The earliest stages of writing date back to the time of the earliest human beings. These forms were very primitive but could be understood by almost anyone, even if the person did not speak the language, because the writing consisted of drawings. The first developed system of writing did not appear until around 3500 B.C. when the Sumerians began to produce written records. Originally, their writing consisted of picturelike symbols scratched out on clay tablets. These were later modified to produce cuneiform script, which used wedge-shaped symbols.

The development of writing continued with the Egyptians' use of picture symbols called hieroglyphics in about 3000 B.C. These symbols stood for whole words or syllables. From this rather complex system, the Semites of Syria worked out an alphabet-type of writing in about 1500 B.C. It used symbols to show consonant sounds like the Egyptians. In about 1000 B.C., the Phoenicians developed a simple system of about 22 signs on which the Greek, Hebrew, Arabic and Sanskrit alphabets are based.

Today, we use the Roman alphabet. The Romans did not invent it. Rather, they improved upon the Greek alphabet, giving most letters their modern form by A.D. 114. Originally, the alphabet consisted of only 20 letters in capital form. By the Middle Ages, the last of the 26 had been added. Small letters developed gradually from capitals.

Teaching Suggestions

- Have students write a poem using each letter in the alphabet to begin a sentence. Students can write about anything they want. Hang students' poems up on the "Awesome Alphabets" bulletin board.
- Several sets of encyclopedias feature an article about each letter of the alphabet. (Each letter begins its alphabetical listing in the encyclopedia.) Assign a different letter of the alphabet to each student. Tell students to prepare a report about the letter and present it to the class. On a piece of posterboard, have each student make the symbol representing his/her letter in the International Flag code, semaphore code, Morse code, Braille and sign language. Display the symbols.
- Lead students in a discussion about the history of writing. Ask students to hypothesize how old writing is, how it began, why it is necessary, how it spread, etc. As a class, make a time line for students to visualize the development of writing. Things to include on the time line:
  1) Thousands of years ago—pictures; 2) 3500 B.C.—Sumerians, first primitive form; 3) 3000 B.C.—Egyptians, hieroglyphics; 4) 1500 B.C.—Semites, alphabet; 5) 1000 B.C.—Phoenicians, alphabet; 6) 800 B.C.—Greeks, alphabet
- Explain to students that most books of writing come from magazines and newspapers that are printed in the Roman alphabet. The Roman alphabet is not really well-suited to writing words in English. It has several symbols with more than one sound, and it does not have separate symbols for every sound. Have students give examples of these kinds of letters.
- Distribute reproduced pages of alphabets. Tell students to try writing their names using the different alphabets.
- Divide students into small groups. Have each group research a subtopic of writing and present its findings to the class. (Suggestions: vocabulary, time line items, pictographs, Hittites, Chinese language, Babylonia, Assyria, etc.)
- Give each student a copy of page 58, *Signature Cylinders*. Go over it with the students. Have them follow the directions to design and make a signature cylinder.

Signature Cylinders

Name _____

Thousands of years ago, if a person could not write, he/she could sign his/her name using a signature cylinder. A cylinder with a design on it rolled onto a piece of clay created a picture that was the person's signature. Make your own signature cylinder following the directions below.

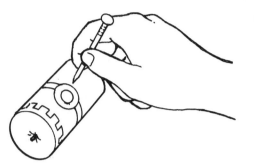

1. Using a nail, carve the design or picture you want as a signature into a candle stub or fat crayon. Carve it on all sides making your carvings fairly deep.

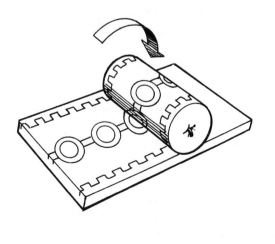

2. Make a flat rectangle from a piece of clay. Use a rolling pin to flatten it to about a one-half inch thickness. The clay should be about 2-3 inches wide and 5-6 inches long.

3. Using a knife, trim off the edges.

4. Roll your signature cylinder over the clay rectangle.

5. Let the clay harden. Your teacher will fire it so that you can use it as a paperweight.

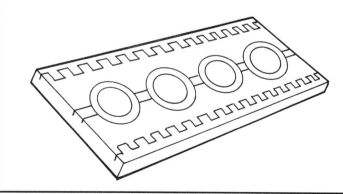

World War I

Concepts

- Boundaries changed and empires dissolved as a result of treaties after World War I.
- Treaties created new nations.
- President Wilson's Fourteen Points were meant to serve as a basis for a peaceful settlement. However, they were largely disregarded by the Allies at the peace conference.

Objectives

- To develop comparison skills
- To recognize that new nations were created and some countries lost land as boundaries were changed after World War I
- To learn about President Wilson's Fourteen Points
- To develop debating skills
- To develop skills in drawing conclusions

Vocabulary

Allies, Alsace-Lorraine, Austria-Hungary, Balkans, Central Powers, colonies, covenant, international waters, nationalism, Ottoman Empire, reparation, Versailles

Materials

world maps before and after World War I, summary of Wilson's Fourteen Points (page 60), copies of *Synopsis of Peace Treaties* (page 61) for students

Preparation

- Make a large copy of Wilson's Fourteen Points (summarized) on page 60 to hang in your classroom.
- Make a copy of activity page 61, *Synopsis of Peace Treaties*, for each student.

Background Information

World War I was fought between the Allies (Belgium, France, Great Britain, Serbia, the United States, and Russia) and the Central Powers (Germany, Austria-Hungary and the Ottoman Empire). Both sides expected a quick victory. Instead, the war lasted over four years. It left Europe exhausted and many governments weakened. The peace treaties involved were either not signed or signed under protest by many nations. Some historians believe it is these treaties that eventually led to World War II.

Teaching Suggestions

- Display a map of the world before World War I next to a map of the world after World War I. Have students compare the maps and recognize what countries/empires existed before and after the war. Let groups of students make lists of their comparisons to present to the class.
- Discuss the vocabulary. Have students locate the places listed and research their role in World War I.
- Review some facts about World War I with students including when it started (1914); some of its causes (assassination of Archduke Francis Ferdinand—heir to Austria-Hungarian throne—and his wife Sophie; feelings of nationalism; military alliances among countries; secret diplomacy by governments); who its first participants were (Central Powers—Austria-Hungary, Germany, Ottoman Empire; Allies—Belgium, France, Great Britain, Russia and Serbia); where the war was fought (Belgium, France, Germany, Austria-Hungary, Russia, Romania); when the United States entered (April 6, 1917); how long the war lasted (over four years); etc.
- Have students write a report about a specific feature or person involved in World War I. Add your suggestions to the list below.
    Georges Clemenceau
    Flanders Field
    David Lloyd George
    Paul von Hindenburg
    The Battle of Jutland
    League of Nations
    Lusitania
    Nicholas II of Russia
    Ottoman Empire
    John J. Pershing
    Battles of Verdun
    War Aces
    Wilhelm II
    Woodrow Wilson
    Count von Zeppelin

- Present the summary of Wilson's Fourteen Points to students (page 60). Explain that he introduced this set of principles ten months before the war ended. He meant for them to be used as a guide for a peaceful settlement. Review each point and its meaning with your students. (The first five established general ideals. The next eight dealt with immediate political and territorial problems. The last point established an association of nations to help keep world peace.) Then, divide students into pairs. Assign one of Wilson's Fourteen Points to each pair. Have each student take an opposite side of the point and debate it.
- Have students complete a Venn diagram comparing World War I to another of the wars the United States has been involved in.
- Give each student a copy of page 61, *Synopsis of Peace Treaties*. Have a student read each one aloud and discuss it as a class. Ask students how much consideration was given to Wilson's Fourteen Points. Ask students if the treaties strengthened or weakened the new governments, which country was the most severely punished, etc. See if the students think the punishment was just, too harsh or not harsh enough. Have students give reasons for their opinions and state other possible alternatives there could have been if they don't agree with the punishment. Tell students that some historians believe that these treaties were a cause for World War II. Ask what their opinion is and why. Have a student read the last paragraph on the page. Tell students to complete the page. If they need more writing space, they should use the back of the paper.

The Fourteen Points

History

Name _____

President Wilson announced his Fourteen Points in a speech before the U.S. Congress on January 8, 1918. He had hoped they would be used as a guide for peace settlement.

1. Open covenants of peace openly arrived at, with no secret international agreements in the future.

2. Freedom of the seas outside territorial waters in peace and in war, except in case of international action to enforce international treaties.

3. Removal of all possible economic barriers and establishment of equal trade conditions among nations.

4. Reduction of national armaments to the lowest point consistent with domestic safety.

5. Free, open-minded, and absolutely impartial adjustment of all colonial claims.

6. Evacuation of German troops from all Russian territory, an opportunity for Russia independently to determine its own political development and national policy, and a welcome for Russia into the society of free nations.

7. Evacuation of German troops from Belgium and the rebuilding of that nation.

8. Evacuation of German troops from all French territory and the return of Alsace-Lorraine to France.

9. Readjustment of Italian frontiers along the clearly recognizable lines of nationality.

10. Limited self-government for the peoples of Austria-Hungary.

11. Evacuation of German troops from Romania, Serbia, and Montenegro, and independence guaranteed for the Balkan countries.

12. Independence for Turkey, but an opportunity to develop self-government for other nationalities under Turkish rule, and guarantees that the Dardanelles be permanently opened as a free passage to ships of all nations.

13. Independence for Poland.

14. "A general association of nations must be formed under specific covenants for the purpose of affording mutual guarantees of political independence and territorial integrity to great and small states alike."

Synopsis of Peace Treaties

History

Name _____

Below are five treaties which together are known as the Peace of Paris.

Treaty of Versailles

This treaty marked the official end of World War I. It was signed by Germany and 32 allied countries. The treaty blamed Germany for the war and imposed reparations to be paid by Germany to the Allies for the damages the war had incurred. It also gave away much territory the Germans considered theirs. Under the treaty, Germany's military forces were also reduced. Germany's post war government was weakened.

Treaty of Saint Germain

This treaty was signed by the Allies and by the Republic of Austria. It gave complete independence to Hungary, Czechoslovakia, Poland and Yugoslavia. It also prohibited Austria from uniting with Germany and reduced the size of Austria's army.

Treaty of Trianon

This treaty was between the Western Allies and Hungary. It called for the reduction in the size and population of Hungary. Hungary lost its access to the sea and some of its natural resources. The size of its army was reduced.

Treaty of Sèvres

This treaty was between the Allies and Turkey. In it, the Ottoman Empire was abolished. Turkey's borders were redefined and it became a much smaller country. An allied commission was also established to control the Turkish economy.

Treaty of Neuilly

This treaty was between the Allies and Bulgaria. In it, Bulgaria ceded some of its territory to Greece and Yugoslavia. Bulgaria also agreed to pay reparations and to limit the size of its army.

The U.S. Senate did not ratify the Treaty of Versailles because it included the covenant of the League of Nations. Many members of the Senate felt that the League of Nations would lead to unwanted American involvement in European disputes. Write if you agree or disagree with what the Senate did and give reasons for your opinion.

_____

_____

_____

_____

_____

World War II

Concepts

- Political unrest and poor economic conditions brought dictators to power in the 1930's.
- Almost every part of the world was affected by World War II.
- World War II caused great devastation.
- Propaganda is a manipulative communication tool.

Objectives

- To understand the far-reaching effect World War II had on people and their countries
- To learn about dictatorship
- To understand the power of propaganda
- To develop interpretive skills

Vocabulary

Axis, communism, fascism, Nazism, propaganda

Materials

world map, copies of activity pages 64 and 65, *Words From World War II Figures*

Preparation

Make copies of activity pages 64 and 65, *Words From World War II Figures,* for students.

Background Information

The 1930's were plagued by political unrest and poor economic conditions. Strong political movements developed. Japan, Italy and Germany became aggressive in their goal of territorial expansion. The people of these distressed nations looked to strong leaders to rid their countries of problems. Dictatorship seemed an easy answer, and so dictators rose to power.

The ravages of World War II were devastating. More people were killed, more property was destroyed and more lives were disrupted than in any other war in history. At the end of the war, Western Europe was no longer the world power it had been. The United Nations was established to keep peace in the world. It was hoped that there would never be another war, but history speaks for itself.

Teaching Suggestions

- Review some of the causes of World War II by asking students some of the questions below.

1. Which countries that were victorious in World War I were dissatisfied with World War I's peace treaties? Why? What did they do about it? (Italy and Japan felt they couldn't compete with other nations for markets, raw materials and colonies; They looked for lands to conquer to get what they considered their share of the world's resources and markets.)

2. Why were the losers dissatisfied? (They did not like peace settlements.) How did they behave? (Poor economic conditions led people to look to dictators for answers to their problems.)

3. What were some extreme political movements in the late 1920's and '30's? What were the principles of each? (**Nazism**—Germany - tightly restricted personal freedom but allowed private ownership of property; aggressive anti-Semitism, nationalism, militarism and expansion of Germany's borders; opposed democracy, communism, socialism and other political systems which favored equality; **Militarism**—Warrior class seen in the highest regard. War and conquests were the highest human achievements. Slogan of militarists: Bringing the Eight Corners of the World Under One Roof; **Communism**—Standard of living is generally lower; goals of their party are more important than individual rights and liberties; people who criticize Communist leaders are punished; no magazines,

newspapers, etc., which oppose communism are allowed; religious worship is discouraged; **Fascism**—government usually headed by a dictator; total government control of political, economic, cultural, religious and social activities)

4. Why did dictators come into power in the 1930's? (People looked to these dictators to help them out of poor economic conditions.)

5. What kind of person was Hitler? Mussolini? Stalin? Give reasons for your opinions. (**Hitler**—controlled Germany from 1933-45; anyone who opposed him was executed or jailed; responsible for death of many Jews; **Mussolini**—founded Fascism and ruled Italy from about 1922-45; enslaved Italians; kept control by means of murder, exile and prison camps; **Stalin**—dictator of former U.S.S.R. from 1929-53; allowed no opposition to his decisions: executed or jailed those who helped him to power because he was threatened by them; killed millions of Soviet peasants who opposed government control of farms; People hated him.)

6. Why couldn't the League of Nations keep world peace? (The most powerful nations couldn't agree on the main purpose of the League. Not all friendly nations belonged.)

- Continue discussing World War II. Ask some of the questions below and on page 63 plus some of your own to help students understand who was involved in the conflict.

1. When did the war begin? (September 1, 1939) What signaled its beginning? (Attack of Poland by Germany)

2. Who were the Axis? (nine countries—See encyclopedia.) Allies? (about 50 countries—See encyclopedia.)

3. Which countries/territories fell to Germany? (Poland, Denmark,

History

World War II continued

Teaching . . . continued

Norway, Belgium, Luxembourg, Netherlands, France, Yugoslavia, Greece, Austria, Czechoslovakia) to Italy? (Ethiopia, Albania) to Japan? (Burma, Netherlands East Indies, Malaysia, Philippines, Thailand, Singapore, Guam and Wake Islands, New Britain, New Ireland, Admiralty Islands, Solomon Islands) Look at a world map to locate them.

4. What were the initial feelings of the United States toward involvement in the war? (U.S. remained neutral. Many did not want the U.S. to go to war.) Why did it change its opinion? (The Japanese attacked Pearl Harbor.)

- Ask students what some of the hardships of war were for military and civilian populations.
- Have students write reports on various people and events surrounding World War II including battles, military and political leaders, conferences and treaties, and more specific topics like concentration camps, the Gestapo, holocaust, Nuremberg Trials, etc.
- Ask students to compare the weapons used in World War II with those used in World War I. Then, have students compare them with weapons today. Ask students how weather can often be used as a "weapon." You could have students compare any number of things using a Venn diagram. They could compare two or three wars and their weapons, geographical locations, causes, results, treaties, etc.
- Ask students how the atomic bomb affected the war and the future of the world. Ask students if they feel President Truman made the right decision to use it. Have students write essays defending their opinions.
- Invite some people who remember World War II to speak to your class about life as a civilian

or in the military. Ask them to include subjects like rationing, patriotism, women going to war, battles, etc. To further stimulate students' interest, invite veterans from other wars the U.S. has been involved in.

- If there is a war memorial in your town, visit it. Talk about memorials of World War II—the *U.S.S. Arizona*, the U.S. Marine Corps War Memorial, etc. Discuss memorials of other wars (Tomb of the Unknowns, Vietnam Veterans Memorial, *U.S.S. Constitution*, etc.).
- Discuss symbols of World War II: Churchill's "V"—famous victory salute (fingers formed into a "V"); the swastika (Nazi emblem); "Rosie the Riveter" (term used for women who took men's places in plants which produced war materials); Uncle Sam posters (asked men and women to work in World War II defense plants).
- Tell students that propaganda was employed by all the warring nations to 1) win support for their policies, 2) spread their beliefs and 3) relate information—sometimes the truth, sometimes not—about the progress of the war. Ask students if they can think of any instances now in which propaganda is used. Have them look for examples in newspapers or listen for it on newscasts.
- Present a local issue to students. Have students choose a side of the issue and write propaganda to support it. Have students read it to the class. Ask the class to decide if what has been written is believable.

For extra fun, students could write and illustrate propaganda for both sides of an issue.

- Ask students the names of leaders they associate with the war on either side. Then, give each student copies of activity pages 64 and 65, *Words From World War II Figures*. Explain to students that some of the people you mentioned spoke and/or wrote memorable words. Have students

read the quotations on these pages and write their interpretations of them.

- Assign students countries which were involved in World War II. Have students write reports on conditions in their assigned countries before, during and after the war.
- Have students pretend they are living during one of the wars the U.S. has been involved in. Have them keep a diary for several days in which they write about their experiences.

Notes/Ideas for Next Time

_____
_____
_____
_____
_____
_____
_____
_____
_____
_____
_____
_____
_____
_____
_____
_____
_____
_____
_____
_____
_____
_____
_____
_____
_____
_____

Words From World War II Figures

History

Name _____

Below are some memorable quotations spoken by some very famous people during World War II. Read each quote and write your interpretation of it on the lines below it.

Franklin Roosevelt

Fourth Inaugural Address—January 20, 1945:

"We have learned that we cannot live alone, at peace; that our own well-being is dependent on the well-being of other nations, far away. We have learned that we must live as men, and not as ostriches, nor as dogs in the manger. We have learned to be citizens of the world, members of the human community."

_____

_____

_____

_____

The following address was written for Jefferson Day broadcast April 13, 1945, but was never delivered. Roosevelt died April 12, 1945:

"More than an end to war, we want an end to the beginnings of all wars."

_____

_____

_____

_____

Fireside Chat—February 23, 1942:

"Never before have we had so little time in which to do so much."

_____

_____

_____

_____

Joseph Stalin

Address to the Moscow Soviet—November 6, 1942:

"The Hitlerite blackguards . . . . have turned Europe into a prison of nations, and this they call the new order in Europe."

_____

_____

_____

_____

History

Words From World War II Figures continued

Name _____

Adolph Hitler

Attributed remark, prior to the invasion of Poland (1939):

"Never tolerate the establishment of two continental powers in Europe."

_____

_____

_____

Winston Churchill

Address at Harrow School—October 29, 1941:

"Do not let us speak of darker days; let us speak rather of sterner days. These are not dark days: these are great days—the greatest days our country has ever lived; and we must all thank God that we have been allowed, each of us according to our stations, to play a part in making these days memorable in the history of our race."

_____

_____

_____

_____

Speech to the Canadian Senate and House of Commons—December 30, 1941:

"We have not journeyed all this way across the centuries, across the oceans, across the mountains, across the prairies, because we are made of sugar candy."

_____

_____

_____

Harry Truman

To reporters the day after he became President—April 13, 1945:

"When they told me yesterday what had happened, I felt like the moon, the stars and all the planets had fallen on me."

_____

_____

_____

Address to nation announcing atomic bomb—August 6, 1945:

"Sixteen hours ago an American airplane dropped one bomb on Hiroshima . . . .The force from which the sun draws its power has been loosed against those who brought war to the Far East."

_____

_____

_____

Progressive Movement

Concepts

- Economic, political and social changes may be brought about when wretched or corrupt economic, political and social conditions exist.
- Citizens can mandate economic, political and social changes.
- Without mandated economic, political or social changes, conditions may remain the same or even deteriorate.
- Economic, political and social change is ongoing.

Objectives

- To learn that economic, political and social changes are brought about by need
- To realize that citizen mandates may be a force to bring about change
- To realize that unsatisfactory conditions that are left alone may not change or may even deteriorate
- To become aware of needs in current economic, political and social conditions

Vocabulary

conservative, corruption, monopoly, muckraker, progressive, reform

Materials

newspapers, political and economic magazines, editorial cartoons, opaque projector, one copy of page 67 per student

Preparation

Cut out letters that read: **Economic, Political, Social Problems**. Put them on a bulletin board. Cut out and save editorial cartoons involving these topics.

Background Information

Industry had grown so fast during the 1800's that it caused many problems like business monopolies, corrupt politics, slums and poor working conditions in factories and mines. A progressive movement began in America during a nationwide depression that lasted from about 1893 to 1897. Many reformers worked to relieve the problems. They called themselves "progressives." The movement lasted until 1917 when America entered World War I.

Teaching Suggestions

- Write the following headings at the top of three columns on a bulletin board: **Economic, Political** and **Social**. List with students some reforms for which the progressives were responsible during the progressive movement. (**Economic**—increased government regulation of business and instituted a series of tax reforms; **Social**—improved the living and working conditions of the poor; **Political**—Mayors worked to end corruption in law enforcement, public transportation and other city services; Political power of voters increased; home rule was granted to many cities, etc.)
- Lead students in a discussion of what living conditions in America might be like if these reforms (and others) had not occurred. Ask students if they think the living conditions in the United States are appropriate for everyone. Have students gather information on the homeless in our country and prepare a report.
- Divide students into as many groups as you have topics (i.e. health, education, crime, deficits, employment, etc.). The topics may be on the local, state or federal level. The topics you select will depend on what is currently happening statewide or nationally. Assign a topic to each group. Each group should look through newspapers and magazines for articles associated with its topic. Instruct groups to cut out the articles and present them to the class. As a class, decide if each article indicates that an economic, political or social change is needed. Discuss what these changes could be. Have each group write the changes it would like to see made concerning the articles it contributes. Put the articles on the bulletin board under the appropriate column.

- Display some editorial cartoons. Explain to students that they are like illustrated letters to the editor. Some are serious about, and others poke fun at, current events or situations. Most are statements. Have students bring in their own editorial cartoons. Or, for more fun, have students create their own as they relate to current problems.

- Discuss muckrakers with the students. (Muckrakers were writers who exposed social and political injustices in the nation. Their work helped bring about many reforms.) As you distribute activity page 67, *Letter to the Editor*, explain to students that, as they have seen, there are current economic, political or social conditions that need to be reformed. Have students look through the articles on the bulletin board and select one to write about in a letter to the editor of the paper.

  Tell students that they are to identify the condition with which they are concerned and its level (local, state, federal). After that, tell students that they should act like a muckraker and write a letter to the editor stating the problem, why a reform is needed, and suggestions for the reform. They should draw an editorial cartoon that shows something about the problem. Put their work up on the bulletin board. Select some to send to local newspapers.

- Divide students into groups. Have each group prepare a TV show entitled, "Muckraking Madness." Students should report on current problems and should have interviews, interviewees, experts, etc. Set a time limit for the shows. Videotape if possible.

- Have groups of students research different countries to find out what kinds of progressive changes might benefit them.

History

Letter to the Editor

Name _____

Condition needing reform: _____

_____

Write a letter to the editor. State the problem, reform needed and suggestions on how reform might be accomplished.

★★★ *The Bugle* ★★★

LETTER TO THE EDITOR

_____

_____

_____

_____

_____

_____

_____

_____

_____

_____

_____

_____

_____

_____

_____

_____

_____

_____

_____

Revolutions

Concepts

- A revolution usually refers to a fundamental change in a nation's government.
- Not all revolutions are violent.
- There are different kinds of revolutions.
- People's dissatisfaction of certain conditions can cause a revolution.

Objectives

- To understand what a revolution is
- To understand that revolutions are carried out in different ways
- To understand that there are different kinds of revolutions
- To understand that different circumstances may cause different revolutions

Vocabulary

rebellion, revolution, revolutionary, riot, warfare

Materials

whistle, encyclopedias, history books, specific books about revolutions, 3" x 5" index cards, large sheet of butcher paper

Preparation

On a large sheet of butcher paper, make a time line similar to the one at the bottom of the page including the Industrial, American, French and Russian revolutions. Color each revolution a different color. Put the time line up in the room. Students will be adding to it later.

Make enough copies of activity page 70, *Revolution Record,* for every student. Divide students into four groups. On every sheet going to one group, write **American Revolution** on the line after "Revolution." On another set, write **Industrial Revolution**; on the third set, write **French Revolution**; and on the last set of papers, write **Russian Revolution**. At the bottom of the activity page under "special report," write the lists below on the appropriate sets of papers. You may want to add some more topics to each list.

American Revolution
Second Continental Congress
Nathan Hale
George Washington
Benedict Arnold
Thomas Paine
King George III

Industrial Revolution
textile industry
child labor
coal (history and use of)
factories
mass production
sweatshop

French Revolution
the National Assembly
Versailles
King Louis XVI
Robespierre
Napoleon Bonaparte
Bastille

Russian Revolution
(The October Revolution)
communism
czars
Leon Trotsky
Bolsheviks
V.I. Lenin
Alexander F. Kerensky

Background Information

Revolutions bring about change. This change can be political, social, economical or cultural and usually affects each of these areas in the end. Revolutions may be led by a group of people dissatisfied with the way things are or they may evolve due to dreadful conditions. In either case, a new system usually ends up replacing the old.

Revolutions throughout history have occurred for different reasons, and their outcomes have resulted in different kinds of change. For example, the Industrial Revolution changed the western world from a rural to an urban society. The American Revolution changed the country's political system. The French Revolution changed the French government and the structure of its society. The Russian Revolution changed the economic and political structure of the country.

Teaching Suggestions

Before doing this activity, speak to three students whom you know won't say anything to spoil the simulation and will be able to carry it off. Tell them that soon after class begins on (name day), you are going to give a very heavy-duty, unreasonable assignment. When they sense the class' dissatisfaction (or at a signal from you), they should stand up and call out, "Unfair! You can't do this!" etc. They should try to get some of the class to go along with them in objecting to the assignment. Also tell them that when you feel there has been enough of a demonstration, you will blow a whistle. Tell them you will need their help and leadership in settling the group down.

	INDUSTRIAL REVOLUTION					
	American Revolution	French Revolution				Russian Revolution
1770	1775	1783	1789	1799	1870	1917 1921

Revolutions continued

Teaching . . . continued

- Begin your class routine as usual. Then, start giving students a really long assignment, due in a short period of time. Lay it on thick until the three students you have chosen begin to oppose you. Resist them, but allow time to continue and draw in other students. When the students' dissatisfaction has been sufficiently demonstrated, blow a whistle, flash the lights or do some other attention-getting technique. Quiet the class. Have them take their seats.

  Ask the class what just happened and why. Explain that this was a mini-revolution. Ask students what a revolution is.

- Discuss the rest of the vocabulary. Then, have students research events like the Haymarket Riot, Boston Tea Party, Shays' Rebellion, Watts riots, Los Angeles riots (Rodney King), etc. Ask students if these were revolutions or not and ask them why they answered as they did. Have students come up with examples of revolutions, riots, acts of terrorism, etc. Students should state the reasons for these events and if they agree with them or not.

- Ask students what some causes for revolutions in history have been. List them on the board under the following headings: **Political**, **Social**, **Economic**, **Cultural**. Explain to students that a revolution can have more than one cause.

- If there are any revolutions occurring in the world at this time, have students look for newspaper and magazine articles and listen to the news for reports of them.

- Divide students into four equal groups. Assign one of the following revolutions to each group: American, French, Russian, Industrial. Give each student in the appropriate group a copy of the *Revolution Record*. Explain that although they may work as a group, each student is to complete his/her own activity sheet.

  Tell students that they are to learn all they can about their assigned revolution. When each student in the group has written three other things that were happening in the world at the time of the revolution, they should pick five different ones, copy them on index cards and put them on the time line under the correct year. Then, explain to students the "special report" at the bottom of the page. Tell students that they are to cover most of the topics listed within each group. They may work alone or in small subgroups. The report should be presented creatively to the class. For example, if students report on a person involved in a specific revolution, they could dress like that person and give a speech pretending to be that person.

- Arrange for a trip to an art or history museum. Look at pictures, crafts, clothes or furniture typical of each revolution's time.

- Have groups of students make up a skit involving a revolution, riot, act of terrorism, etc. It could be modeled after one that has actually taken place or it could relate to an issue facing people today. It can involve the U.S. or a different country. See if the other students can figure out what is happening in each skit. Encourage students to use props (i.e. signs, flags, etc.) to help get their meaning across.

- Tell students to pretend that they are living during a historical revolution that has occurred. Let students choose the revolution and write a story describing their experience.

- Assign groups of students a country. Have the groups research their country to find out what kinds of revolutions, riots, acts of terrorism, etc., have taken place there. Have students prepare a report on it and present it to the class.

Notes/Ideas for Next Time

_____
_____
_____
_____
_____
_____
_____
_____
_____
_____
_____
_____
_____
_____
_____
_____
_____
_____
_____
_____
_____
_____
_____
_____
_____
_____
_____
_____
_____
_____
_____
_____
_____
_____
_____
_____
_____
_____
_____
_____
_____
_____
_____

Revolution Record

History

Name _____

Revolution _____

When it took place _____ Where it took place _____

Kind of revolution (political, social, cultural) _____

Causes of the revolution _____

_____

_____

_____

How was it carried out? _____

_____

_____

_____

What were its outcomes? _____

_____

_____

_____

Write three other things that were happening in the world at the time of this revolution. Include dates. _____

_____

_____

_____

_____

Do a "special report" about a specific person or concern related to the revolution you have just studied. Select one of the following suggestions on which to do a creative review: a conversation, diorama, speech, dramatization, etc. You may work alone or with members of your group. Plan your "special report" below and on another sheet of paper.

_____

_____

_____

_____

_____

_____

_____

GEORGE WASHINGTON

Architecture

Concepts

- Architecture is an old art form.
- Buildings should work efficiently for those who use them.
- A building that works for one may not work for another.

Objectives

- To be aware of different styles of architecture
- To understand that architecture is a reflection of the culture it serves
- To understand that different buildings have different functions

Vocabulary

architecture, beam, blueprint, concrete, dormer, facade

Materials

architectural books and magazines, brads, manila folders, paper punch, typing paper, one copy of page 73 per student

Preparation

- For the students' safety, make arrangements with the physical education teacher to help you with the first four teaching suggestions.
- Put up a "Styles of Architecture" bulletin board. On it, display pictures of different kinds of architecture (i.e. Greek, Romanesque, etc.). Label each style and write its approximate time period. Sources for pictures might be postcards from museums or photocopies from architectural books.
- Ask the school and/or community library to put together a collection of books about architecture. Make an architectural library in your classroom. Take an "architecture walk" of a given area on which you plan to take your class. Prepare a worksheet that pertains to the walk and includes what the students should look for.
- Arrange a trip to an art museum or the office of an architect.

Background Information

Architecture existed over 5,000 years ago in Mesopotamia and Egypt. It has been part of almost every culture since then. A building tells something about the needs and sophistication of a society.

What goes into a building depends on what it is meant to do. Though a building might be attractive on the outside, it is not a well-designed structure if it does not serve well those who use it. Unlike most artists who work alone, an architect does not. An architect must work with his/her clients so that their needs and requirements are met.

Teaching Suggestions

- Invite six students to build a human pyramid. Talk about its structure, where it is strongest and why.
- Have ten students build a human pyramid. Ask the students in the middle and on the bottom what they feel.
- Tell students to pick a partner who is more-or-less equal in weight and size. Have them stand facing each other about three or four feet apart. Tell them to put their arms up in front of them shoulder high, with hands flexed back, and to lean toward each other with straight legs and body until their palms touch. While they hold this position, have the students talk about what they feel and what their body shape from the side is called. (profile)

- Have the partners stand side-by-side about one or two feet apart. Tell them to hold inside hands firmly together and to lean away from each other letting their bodies fall to the outside.

Have students talk about what they feel. Notice if their outside arms are extended and ask why that (probably) happened.

- Tell students to take their seats. Comment that the stresses they felt (pushed, pulled, squeezed, etc.) are "felt" in buildings, too. Architects' plans allow for such stress. Ask students how a pyramid is like a building. Ask them when a building might experience the same pressures the students felt when they leaned toward and away from each other.
- Have students pretend that they are going to build a house. Have them jot down what they would want in the house. Have some students read aloud what they listed. Make the comment that many of the students' wants and needs for their house were different.
- Discuss different types of buildings (i.e. movie theaters, office buildings, supermarkets, etc.) and if any can be interchanged with each other and still serve the same purpose.
- Lead a discussion about the aspects of architecture. Ask students what they think an architect considers when he/she designs a building. Ask students what things an architect must specifically consider when designing certain buildings (i.e. art gallery, restaurant, bank, etc.).
- Point out the "Styles of Architecture" bulletin board. Explain to students that a society's architecture reflects the values and way of life of its people. Ask students if they think architecture changed after the Industrial Revolution in the United States,

Architecture continued

Teaching . . . continued

and if so why. (Yes—needed new buildings to accommodate new technology.) Explain to students that the Industrial Revolution marked the evolution of modern architecture which continues today. Ask students if they know what one of the greatest contributions modern architecture made in this period and when it was made. (the skyscraper in 1890's)

- Assign each student a type of architecture to study in depth. (Suggestions of topics: *Early Architecture*—Mesopotamian, Egyptian; *Asian and Pre-Columbian*—Chinese, Japanese, Indian, Islamic, Pre-Columbian; *Classical*—Minoan, Mycenaean, Classical Greek, Roman; *Medieval*—Early Christian, Byzantine, Carolingian, Romanesque, Gothic; Renaissance; Baroque; *1700's*—Rococo, Palladian, Neoclassical, Colonial American; *1800's*—Industrial Revolution, Greek revival, Gothic revival; *Modern Architecture*—Europe, America; etc.) Tell them that they are to do individual reports even though two or three students may have the same period. Explain that they are not only to include the style of architecture at this time, but also what life was like during the period. With the students, list on the board the kind of information they should include in their report (i.e. vocabulary of their architectural style, illustrations, values, occupations, living conditions, clothes, values, etc.).

Show students how they will present their report in booklet form. Tell students that they may write on regular notebook paper or use typing paper. Then, they are to put the papers together in a manila folder, punch two holes, and hold it together with brads.

- Have a 20-minute reading period during which students may read each other's booklets.

- Take an architectural walk in a neighborhood or in your city. Prepare a worksheet that pertains to the walk and includes clues to what the students should look for. After the walk, ask students what buildings they saw and what their functions were. See if students noticed any buildings that were no longer occupied. Ask them why they think this is so. See if students can identify any specific styles or can tell how old an area is. Ask students why certain materials were used in certain buildings. Have students describe how various buildings illustrated occupants' needs.

- Take a trip to an art museum. Look at paintings of architecture from the various periods.

- Invite an architect to come talk to your class or take your class to an architect's office.

- Give each student a copy of activity page 73, *Get a Clue!* Tell students that they are to write ten clues about a topic related to architecture. Give students the following choices of subjects: style of architecture, famous buildings, famous architects or parts of a building, etc. When students are finished, have them take turns reading their clues out loud, letting the other students guess what the clues describe. Note: You may want to give students a list of the topics used if they are not familiar with all of them.

- Have groups of students work together to compare two styles of architecture. Have students present their information, including pictures, to the class.

- Let students make collages of their favorite style(s) of architecture. Have students identify the buildings they chose and the type of architecture portrayed.

- Have students redesign a famous statue, monument, building, etc. Have them tell why they made the changes they did.

Notes/Ideas for Next Time

_____
_____
_____
_____
_____
_____
_____
_____
_____
_____
_____
_____
_____
_____
_____
_____
_____
_____
_____
_____
_____
_____
_____
_____
_____
_____
_____
_____
_____
_____
_____
_____
_____
_____
_____
_____
_____
_____
_____
_____

Art

Get a Clue!

Name _____

Write ten clues about an architectural-related topic of your choice. The clues could describe a style of architecture, a famous building, a famous architect or a part of a building.

1. _____
_____

2. _____
_____

3. _____
_____

4. _____
_____

5. _____
_____

6. _____
_____

7. _____
_____

8. _____
_____

9. _____
_____

10. _____
_____

Middle Ages

Concepts

- A castle or manor was usually the home and fortress of a nobleman.
- A nobleman spent much of his life defending his kingdom.
- Knights and vassals pledged their loyalty to noblemen and in return often received a fief.

Objectives

- To be aware of social order in the Middle Ages
- To understand reasons for a castle's layout

Vocabulary

chivalry, feudalism, fief, manorialism, Middle Ages, vassal

Materials

books about castles, shirt cardboard or oaktag, ruler, cardboard, X-acto™ knife and/or sharp scissors, glue, empty toilet paper rolls, toothpicks, scraps of paper, papier-mâché paste, bowl, old newspapers, paint, paintbrushes, 12" squares of cardboard, one copy of pages 76-80 per student

Preparation

Make papier-mâché paste. Mix paints. Obtain shirt cardboards and pieces of at least 12" square cardboard. Ask for volunteer help to supervise cutting activity.

Background Information

At one time during the Middle Ages, Europe was divided into many kingdoms. Most of the kingdoms were weak and had little control. As a result, hundreds of noblemen became the supreme rulers of their own fiefs. The castle or manor was the center of each fief. From it, the nobleman ruled his kingdom through a form of government called feudalism. He had judicial, political, economic and military control over the people who lived in the kingdom. Knights who pledged their loyalty to the nobleman received a small fief as payment.

Teaching Suggestions

- Go over the vocabulary with the students. Make them aware of the different levels in medieval society. (kings; noblemen, lords, vassals, knights; peasants)
- Ask students what buildings they associate with the Middle Ages and why. (castles)
- Ask students who they think lived in the castle besides the noblemen. (family, servants, soldiers, etc.)
- Lead a discussion about the rooms in a castle and their necessity. Ask students why a castle would have a storehouse, barracks, great hall, prison, armory, treasure house, etc.
- When a nobleman wasn't in battle, he often sat in the castle's great hall socializing with his knights. Have students write a conversation a nobleman might have had with one of his knights during their merrymaking or while in battle.
- Ask students if they think a castle would be a comfortable place in which to live. Have them explain their opinion.
- Have students write a story about living in an old abandoned castle.
- Give each student a copy of *Creating a Castle* (pages 76-80). Follow the directions for cutting cardboard and demonstrate this for the students. Remind students to read all of the directions before they begin. Students may use the diagrams of the castle on page 75 for help.
- Have students choose an existing castle somewhere in the world and pretend they live there. Students should write stories about their castle and include real facts about the castle.
- Let groups of students perform skits set in the Middle Ages involving noblemen, vassals, knights, peasants, etc. For extra fun, students could throw in a character like Michael Jordan, the President of the United States, George Washington, Oprah Winfrey, Sally Ride, etc. Have students perform the skits for the class.

Notes/Ideas for Next Time

_____
_____
_____
_____
_____
_____
_____
_____
_____
_____
_____
_____
_____
_____
_____
_____
_____
_____
_____
_____
_____
_____
_____
_____
_____
_____
_____
_____
_____
_____
_____
_____
_____
_____
_____
_____

Castle Diagrams

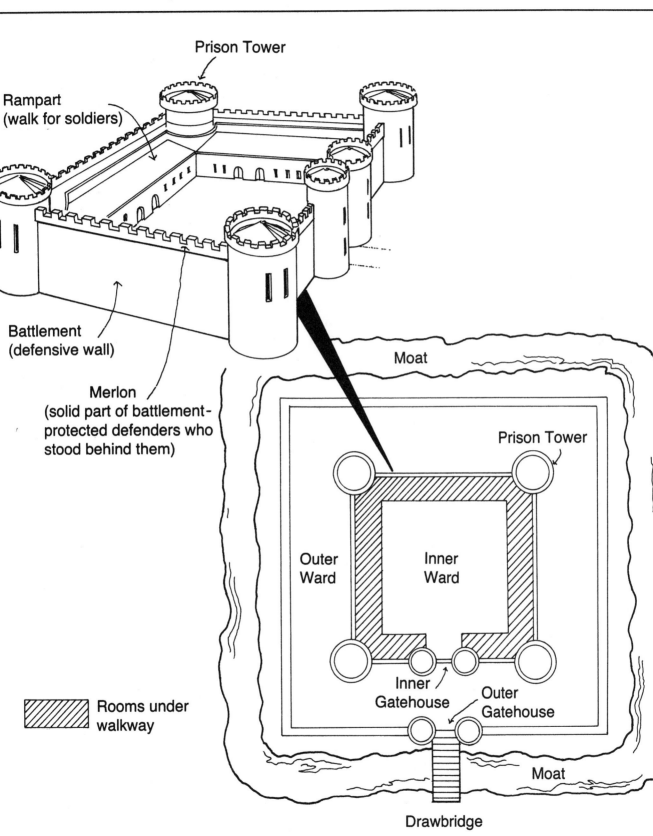

Prison Tower

Rampart
(walk for soldiers)

Battlement
(defensive wall)

Merlon
(solid part of battlement-
protected defenders who
stood behind them)

Rooms under
walkway

Moat

Prison Tower

Outer
Ward

Inner
Ward

Inner
Gatehouse

Outer
Gatehouse

Moat

Drawbridge

Creating a Castle

Make your very own castle by following the directions.

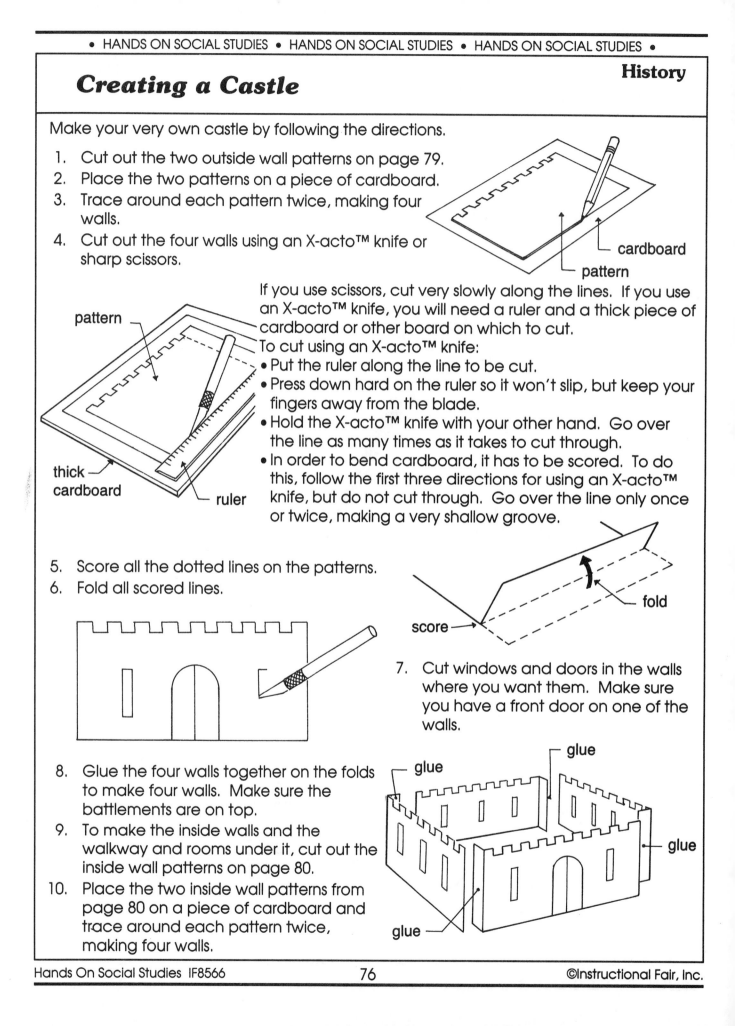

1. Cut out the two outside wall patterns on page 79.
2. Place the two patterns on a piece of cardboard.
3. Trace around each pattern twice, making four walls.
4. Cut out the four walls using an X-acto™ knife or sharp scissors.

cardboard

pattern

pattern

thick cardboard

ruler

If you use scissors, cut very slowly along the lines. If you use an X-acto™ knife, you will need a ruler and a thick piece of cardboard or other board on which to cut.
To cut using an X-acto™ knife:
• Put the ruler along the line to be cut.
• Press down hard on the ruler so it won't slip, but keep your fingers away from the blade.
• Hold the X-acto™ knife with your other hand. Go over the line as many times as it takes to cut through.
• In order to bend cardboard, it has to be scored. To do this, follow the first three directions for using an X-acto™ knife, but do not cut through. Go over the line only once or twice, making a very shallow groove.

5. Score all the dotted lines on the patterns.
6. Fold all scored lines.

score

fold

7. Cut windows and doors in the walls where you want them. Make sure you have a front door on one of the walls.

8. Glue the four walls together on the folds to make four walls. Make sure the battlements are on top.
9. To make the inside walls and the walkway and rooms under it, cut out the inside wall patterns on page 80.
10. Place the two inside wall patterns from page 80 on a piece of cardboard and trace around each pattern twice, making four walls.

glue

glue

glue

glue

History

Creating a Castle continued

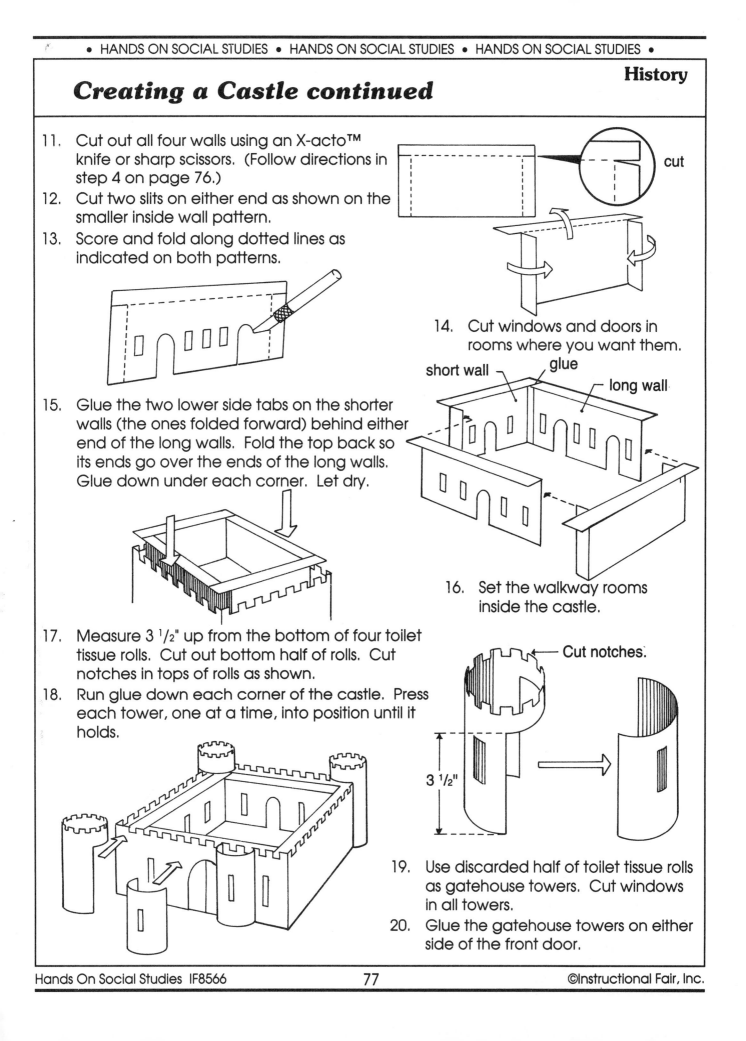

11. Cut out all four walls using an X-acto™ knife or sharp scissors. (Follow directions in step 4 on page 76.)

12. Cut two slits on either end as shown on the smaller inside wall pattern.

13. Score and fold along dotted lines as indicated on both patterns.

cut

14. Cut windows and doors in rooms where you want them.

short wall   glue   long wall

15. Glue the two lower side tabs on the shorter walls (the ones folded forward) behind either end of the long walls. Fold the top back so its ends go over the ends of the long walls. Glue down under each corner. Let dry.

16. Set the walkway rooms inside the castle.

17. Measure 3 ½" up from the bottom of four toilet tissue rolls. Cut out bottom half of rolls. Cut notches in tops of rolls as shown.

18. Run glue down each corner of the castle. Press each tower, one at a time, into position until it holds.

Cut notches.

3 ½"

19. Use discarded half of toilet tissue rolls as gatehouse towers. Cut windows in all towers.

20. Glue the gatehouse towers on either side of the front door.

History

Creating a Castle continued

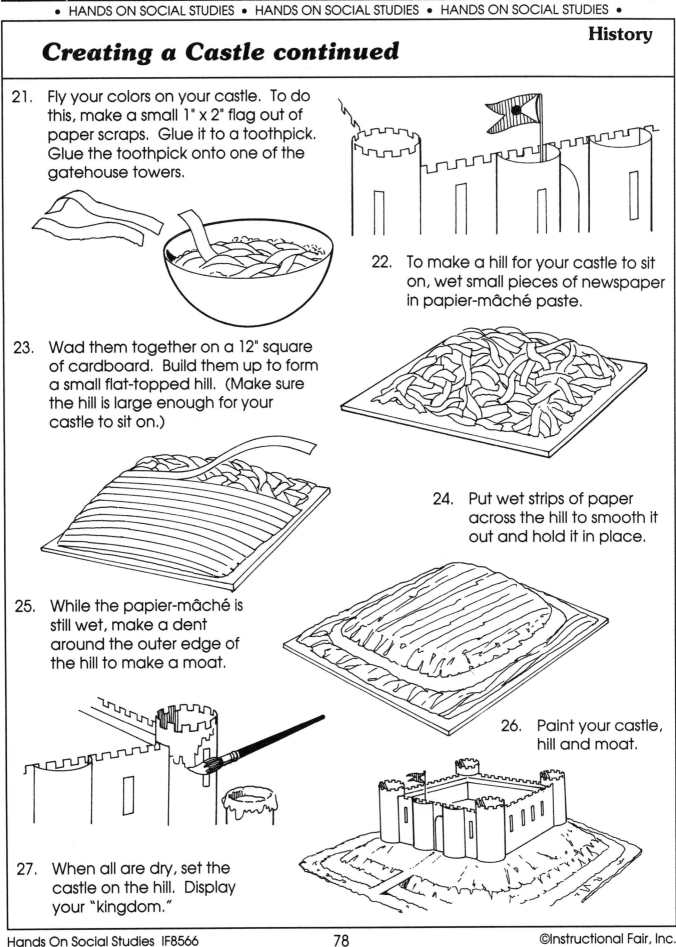

21. Fly your colors on your castle. To do this, make a small 1" x 2" flag out of paper scraps. Glue it to a toothpick. Glue the toothpick onto one of the gatehouse towers.

22. To make a hill for your castle to sit on, wet small pieces of newspaper in papier-mâché paste.

23. Wad them together on a 12" square of cardboard. Build them up to form a small flat-topped hill. (Make sure the hill is large enough for your castle to sit on.)

24. Put wet strips of paper across the hill to smooth it out and hold it in place.

25. While the papier-mâché is still wet, make a dent around the outer edge of the hill to make a moat.

26. Paint your castle, hill and moat.

27. When all are dry, set the castle on the hill. Display your "kingdom."

History

Outside Wall Patterns

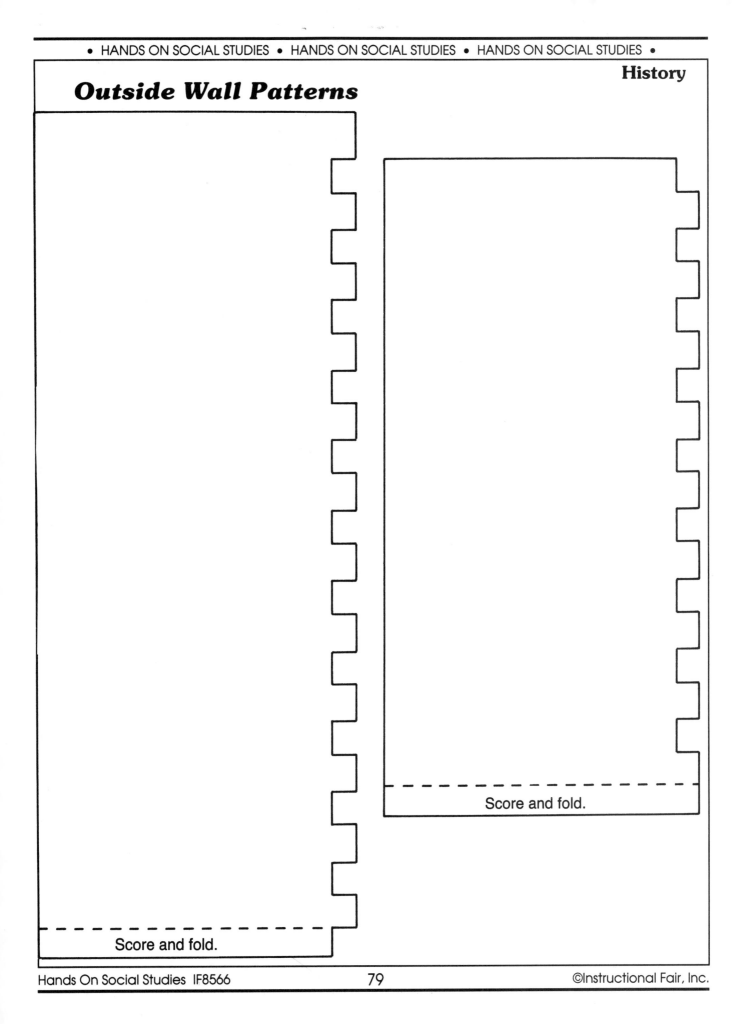

Score and fold.

Score and fold.

Inside Wall Patterns

History

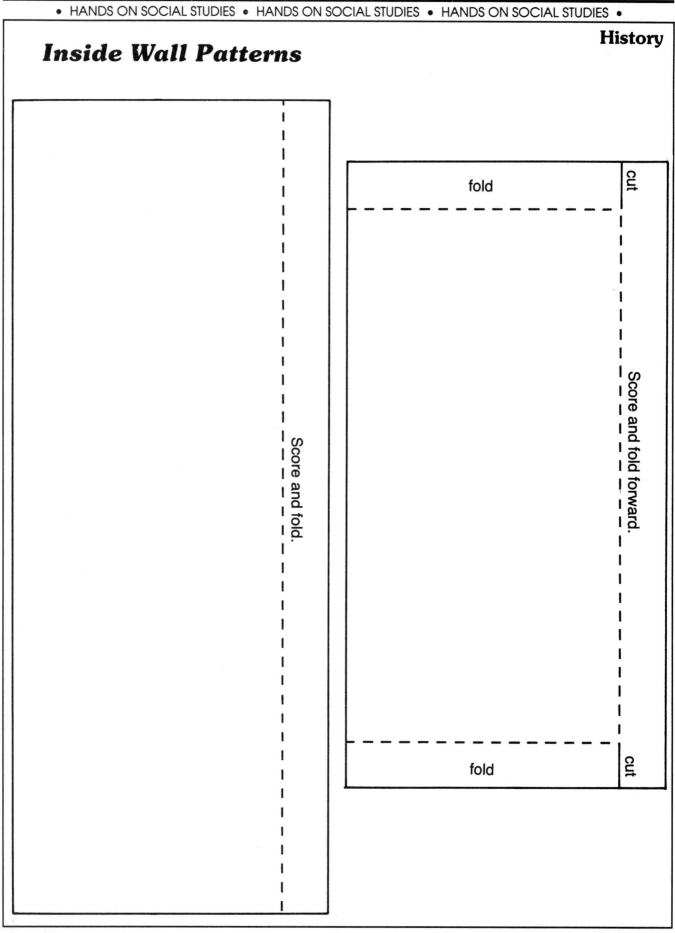

Score and fold.

fold

cut

Score and fold forward.

fold

cut